STRATEGIES FOR JOINT VENTURE SUCCESS

Strategies for
Joint Venture Success

J. Peter Killing

CROOM HELM
London & Canberra

© 1983 J. Peter Killing and Associates Ltd.
Croom Helm Ltd, Provident House, Burrell Row,
Beckenham, Kent BR3 1AT

British Library Cataloguing in Publication Data

Killing J. Peter
    Strategies for joint venture success.
    1. Joint ventures — Management
    I. Title
    658'.049   HD69.17
    ISBN 0-7099-1538-1

Typeset by Mayhew Typesetting, Bristol
Printed and bound in Great Britain by
Biddles Ltd, Guildford and King's Lynn

CONTENTS

LIST OF TABLES

LIST OF FIGURES

To My Parents

PREFACE

When working on a project over a period of years, one becomes sensitised to the subject. Whenever I pick up a newspaper or business magazine, I find that I am scanning for joint venture material. It is certainly not hard to find. As I write this I have a current newspaper clipping in front of me documenting the start-up of four new high technology joint ventures involving Canadian firms. All of the ventures are in North America, and two at least involve substantial amounts of money – $50 million or more. My conclusion after two or three years of monitoring such material is that the joint venture is an organisational form whose time has come.

The joint ventures of the 1980s and 1990s will be, I believe, more important to their parents than has often been the case in the past, which typically saw joint ventures being created in remote developing countries. Many of the new joint ventures are both larger in scale and closer to the hearts of the parents' businesses. Another change I foresee is that managers who currently dislike joint ventures, of whom there are many, will probably find their attitudes changing as they participate in more ventures and thus become better at managing them. I hope that this book will assist in this process. It is based on the experience of managers in both successful and unsuccessful joint ventures and has been written expressly to help managers improve the performance of their joint ventures.

If I am correct in my prediction that joint ventures will become an increasingly prominent feature on the corporate landscape, we will undoubtedly see more studies devoted to their design and management. I hope that this book will provide a useful point of departure for future studies. Work is already under way on the management of such ventures in developing countries, although to the best of my knowledge nothing has yet been done on the management of ventures between corporations and government bodies.

I have been working in the area of joint venture design and management for four or five years now and in that time have obtained help and direction from a lot of people. In the early stages of the project Professors Len Wrigley, Harold Crookell and Tom Poynter helped to shape the study, and later doctoral students Paul Beamish and Jean-Louis Schaan have assisted in sharpening my thoughts. I owe a special debt to Jean-Louis for allowing me to quote at length from his thesis on the management of Mexican ventures, which, as I write this, is in the final stages of completion. But the major acknowledgement must go to the businessmen in Canada, the United States and Europe, who were so willing to talk to a strange Canadian on their doorstep, so that others might learn from their experiences. I was continually delighted and amazed at the openness with which executives were willing to discuss both their successes and their failures; it is that spirit which allows a book like this to be written. For this I thank them.

I have also had a great deal of institutional support. A study like this one is expensive and, as months stretch into years both moral and financial support become important. Housed in the Business School at the University of Western Ontario, I have received plenty of both. Both in the Business School's Fund for Excellence, under the respective administration of research directors Professors David Shaw, John Kennedy and Al Mikalachki, and the Centre for International Business Studies, directed by Professor Harold Crookell, have supported the project from start to finish. Dean C.B. Johnston has also taken a personal interest in my work, helping me bring it to new audiences whenever possible. Special thanks are also due to Pat McCabe, Una Johnston, Nancy Ellery, Jean Fish, Kathy Jillard and Ken Woytaz for managing and producing my various drafts on time and in good humour.

Finally, a note to the people at home. I find that it is difficult to explore new worlds, be they geographical or intellectual, with freedom and confidence without the security of a home base of love and care. For this, thanks to Rebecca and Sarah.

London, Ontario, Canada   J. Peter Killing

1 THE JOINT VENTURE PARADOX

The paradox of joint ventures is simply stated. Although most managers heartily dislike joint ventures, they predict that they will be involved in more and more of them. Indeed, they have already been some startling bursts of activity, as in 1980 when China reportedly signed more than 300 joint venture agreements with foreign firms. Managers also expect that individual ventures are likely to be more important to their firms in the future than they have been in the past. Ventures like the joint engine and transmission plants of Volvo-Peugeot-Renault, and the 1980 Rolls-Royce venture with three Japanese firms to design and manufacture a jet engine for medium distance aircraft are endeavours that reach to the heart of these companies. Their success is critical to the firms involved, far more so than was typically the case with the traditional joint venture used to obtain a share of a growing market in the Third World or otherwise remote country. Peter Drucker has argued that joint ventures will become increasingly important and at the same time states that they are 'the most difficult and demanding of all tools of diversification – and the least understood'.[1] Few executives who have been closely involved with joint ventures would disagree.

The purpose of this book is to help European and North American managers to become more successful with joint ventures. It is based both on a review of existing studies and on a first-hand examination of 35 joint ventures located in North America and Western Europe and two in developing countries. In addition to making observations and conclusions based on interviews with joint venture general managers and executives in their parent companies, I have also written two sets of detailed case studies. Those in Chapter Three examine two joint ventures used to develop techniques for mining the seabed; and in Chapter Seven the failure of two German firms to use joint ventures successfully to exploit their technology in the US market is documented. One other source of information which I have drawn upon is the work of J.L. Schaan. Schaan is a doctoral student working under my direction who is currently completing a thesis which examines the techniques that local and foreign parent companies are using to control joint ventures in Mexico.[2]

In this chapter both sides of the joint venture paradox are examined. We begin with a look at the extent to which joint ventures are being

1

used and the reasons why managers believe this usage rate is likely to increase. Later in the chapter the question of why joint ventures are difficult to manage is addressed — this being the reason why so many managers dislike joint ventures. The chapter ends with the question of whether or not some joint ventures are easier to manage than others.

Who is Using Joint Ventures?

Although there is no complete listing of either joint ventures in existence or of those formed in any given year, it is apparent that many large companies are involved in at least one joint venture. The most recent survey of American firms was done by Alan Janger for the Conference Board and he reported that 'most of the Fortune 500 companies and roughly 40% of industrial companies with more than $100 million sales are engaged in one or more international joint ventures.'[3] Janger's findings are supported by data collected as part of Harvard University's Multinational Enterprise Project, which indicated that as of 1967 only 33 of 187 major US multinational firms did not have at least one international joint venture.[4] Between 1910 and 1967 there was a marked increase in the propensity of these 187 firms to use joint ventures, as the data in Table 1.1 indicate.

Table 1.1: Foreign Manufacturing Subsidiaries. Classified by Multinational Enterprises' Ownership and Period of Entry[a]

| | Multinational Enterprises' Ownership at Time of Entry | | | | | |
| | Wholly owned | | Majority owned | | Minority owned | |
Period of entry	No. of subs.	Percentage of total in period	No. of subs.	Percentage of total in period	No. of subs.	Percentage of total in period
1900–09	48	73.8	16	24.6	1	1.6
1910–19	52	91.2	5	8.8	0	0
1920–9	131	78.4	13	7.8	23	13.8
1930–9	158	75.2	18	8.6	34	16.2
1940–9	115	62.5	18	9.8	51	27.7
1950–4	136	64.8	28	13.3	46	21.9
1955–9	300	62.0	67	13.8	117	24.2
1960–7	780	55.3	260	18.4	371	26.3

Note: a. Excludes subsidiaries in Japan, Spain, Ceylon, India, Mexico, and Pakistan.
Source: J.M. Stopford and L. Wells, *Managing the Multinational Enterprise*, Table 10.1.

As an indicator of what the major firms of the world are doing, these American statistics most likely underestimate the extent to which joint ventures are being used. First, they exclude countries such as Japan in which joint ventures are demanded by the government. Secondly, American firms are generally considered to be less prone to form joint ventures than firms of other nationalities. One study observed, 'Most of the American companies . . . generally resist joint ventures and go to great pains to avoid them . . . Those in European companies do not like joint ventures either . . . however they are markedly less fearful about dealing with "the natives" . . . and seem much more comfortable and able to roll with the punches . . . after they get in'.[5] This observation is supported by the data in Table 1.2, which show that US firms use a lower percentage of joint ventures than firms from most other countries. This is particularly true in developing countries, where, for firms other than American and Swiss, joint ventures are the rule rather than the exception.[6]

To allow a closer look at the way in which joint ventures are being used in a specific industry, I have listed in Table 1.3 joint ventures formed in the automobile industry in a recent two-year period. This record has been compiled from quarterly listings provided by the journal *Mergers and Acquisitions*.[7] As can be seen, 19 ventures were formed during the period, apparently for a wide variety of reasons. Quite a number included government agencies.

Why Use Joint Ventures?

There is not enough evidence available to determine whether or not the rate of joint venture formation is increasing. Janger reported that just over half of the 168 companies in his survey had formed new international joint ventures in the past five years. One third of the total group stated that their rate of international joint venture formation had increased in the past five years.[8] Unfortunately, we do not know what was reported by the other two thirds. The Bureau of Economics of the US Federal Trade Commission does publish an annual listing of joint ventures formed involving American firms, but it is only based on what shows up in the press and other public sources. Also, because the bureau has changed the definition of what it counts as a joint venture, an historical comparison is not possible. One other measure of joint venture formation is found in the listings provided by *Mergers and Acquisitions*,[7] but as with the FTC listings, these are

Table 1.2: Percentage of Foreign Manufacturing Subsidiaries of Large Enterprises Based in Various Parent Countries which were Wholly Owned or Joint Ventures, 1 January 1971 (US data as of 1 January 1968)

National Base of Parent Enterprise	Wholly Owned Subsidiaries[a]	Majority Owned Joint Ventures[b]	Ownership Position: Minority & 50-50 Joint Ventures[c]	Total Number of Subsidiaries Known
	%	%	%	%
In All Countries:				
United States	63	15	22	3,720
United Kingdom	61	19	20	2,236
Japan	9	9	82	445
France	24	29	47	333
Germany	42	28	30	753
Italy	42	24	35	106
Belgium & Luxembourg	37	34	29	184
Netherlands	61	18	20	401
Sweden	64	17	19	155
Switzerland	59	29	19	292
In Less Developed Countries:[d]				
United States	57	19	24	1,583
France	11	37	52	157
Germany	44	31	25	323
Italy	33	25	45	67
Belgium & Luxembourg	21	51	28	39
Netherlands	33	28	39	82
Sweden	39	32	29	44
Switzerland	54	33	26	84

Notes: a. Owned 95% or more by a foreign parent. b. Owned more than 50% but less than 95% by a foreign parent. c. Owned more than 5% but less than 50.01% by a foreign parent. d. 1970 per capita GNP under US $1,200.
Source: Comparative Multinational Enterprise Project, as presented in L.G. Franko, *The European Multinationals*, Table 5.5.

taken from public sources, are primarily American and probably ignore many of the small joint ventures which are formed each year. The number of joint venture formations involving American firms reported by this journal for selected years are shown in Table 1.4. These figures are not reliable enough to support detailed analysis, but generally they suggest that the number of new ventures formed annually by American firms has been constant since 1976, and that roughly one third of these are domestic ventures – formed in the US with US partners. The ventures from which my own sample is primarily taken are the 30–40 per cent of ventures which were formed in Western Europe (with local partners) or in North America with European partners.

Table 1.3: Automobile Industry Joint Ventures, Mid-1978–Mid-1980

(1) August 1978
Bendix Corp. and Renault formed a joint venture to make electrical parts for Renault.

(2) September 1978
Fiat and General Electric formed a joint venture to build a new marine gas turbine engine.

(3) November 1978
Fiat and Peugeot-Citroen formed a joint venture to build a factory in Italy to produce 80,000 light trucks annually, at a cost of 200 billion lira.

(4) November 1978
SAAB-Scania and a Finnish firm formed a joint venture to assemble and import Chryslers into Finland.

(5) February 1979
American Motors and China formed a joint venture to produce four-wheel drive vehicles.

(6) February 1979
Chrysler and the Taiwan Machinery Mfg Co. formed a joint venture to build 10,000 trucks per year in Taiwan.

(7) February 1979
Ford Motor Co. and the ALFA Industrial Group of Mexico formed a joint venture to manufacture aluminium cylinder heads for automotive motors. The plant will cost $52 million.

(8) March 1979
Fiat and SAAB-Scania agreed to develop jointly a new prototype car. The purpose of the joint venture is to limit the costs involved in planning, testing and production of the proposed prototype.

(9) June 1979
Fiat and Versatile Cornat of Canada formed a joint venture to market on a world-wide basis Versatile's four-wheel drive farm tractors.

(10) July 1979
General Motors and Izuzu Motors of Japan formed a joint venture to manufacture cars and trucks in the Philippines. The venture will be 60% owned by GM.

(11) October 1979
Volkswagen, the German Development Co., and a consortium of Egyptian investors will build a joint venture plant in Egypt to produce 10,000 Beetles annually. The venture is expected to cost 50 million marks and will be owned 40% by Volkswagen, 11% by the Development Co. and 49% by the consortium of investors.

(12) November 1979
Ford Motor Company and a Mexican firm formed a venture to build a $47.8 million plant to produce automotive safety glass, 75% of which will be exported. Ford will own 38% of the venture.

(13) January 1980
American Motors, Renault, and a Mexican Company formed a joint venture to manufacture Renault cars which will also be built by AMC in the US. AMC and Renault's combined ownership in the venture will be 25%.

(14) January 1980
Honda Motor and Brazil formed a joint venture to manufacture motorcycles with alcohol-burning engines.

(15) January 1980
Nissan Motor Co. and Motor Iberica, owned by the Spanish Government, formed a joint venture to manufacture trucks in Spain.

Table 1.3 *contd.*

(16) January 1980
   Volkswagen and Peru formed a joint venture to manufacture commercial vehicles and passenger cars in Peru.
(17) April 1980
   General Motors formed a joint venture with Taiwan Machinery Mfg Co. to manufacture heavy duty trucks. Capitalised at $100 million, GM will own 45% of the venture, Taiwan Machinery 35% and the Taiwan Government 20%.
(18) April 1980
   Nissan Motor and a consortium of Taiwanese investors formed a joint venture to produce cars in Taiwan. The venture is owned 45% by Nissan and 55% by the consortium.
(19) June 1980
   Honda Motor Co. and a Yugoslavian firm formed a joint venture to produce engines for agricultural machines. The venture will be capitalised at $4 million.

Source: This information was taken from various issues of *Mergers and Acquisitions: The Journal of Corporate Venture* (produced quarterly by Information for Industry Inc., Virginia, USA.)

Table 1.4: Ventures Involving US Firms

Year	Number Reported	US Ventures with US Partners	US Ventures with Foreign Partners	Western European Ventures	Japanese Ventures	Other
1974	101	22%	12%	20%	12%	38%
1976	166	38%	13%	8%	8%	33%
1978	155	30%	18%	17%	6%	29%
1980	152	33%	18%	20%	7%	22%

To address the question of why managers are predicting that joint venture usage will increase, one needs to understand the reasons why joint ventures are being used now. Janger found that the most common reasons managers gave for entering joint ventures were to develop new markets and gain access to raw materials. But such answers are only half the story. There are other ways of penetrating new markets and getting raw materials. The more significant question is, given that a firm wishes to accomplish these things, why choose a joint venture to do so? Common responses to this question are given below.

1. Government insistence.
2. The project is too large, financially, for either partner to handle alone.
3. Neither firm has all of the skills, typically technical and marketing, to make a success of the business on its own.

4. Only by combining forces can the joint venture partners achieve satisfactory economies of scale in research and development, production, or marketing.

Many governments have been increasing pressure on foreign companies to participate in local joint ventures rather than establish wholly owned subsidiaries. This trend has been most pronounced in developing countries but is currently becoming a factor in developed countries as well. Canada and France, for example, are two countries in which foreign firms find significant hurdles in the way of direct foreign investment. It seems likely that such nationalism will continue to grow, and that an increasing number of joint ventures will be established because of government pressure.

Another factor leading to an increase in joint venture usage is the fact that many projects are getting so large that single firms cannot accept the financial risk which they entail. Exploiting Canada's oil sands and developing the next generation of jet aircraft are two which come to mind. With respect to the latter, a current article observes that there is actually a competition for joint venture partners in the aircraft manufacturing business, because there is simultaneously both a high need for financial risk sharing and a desire to blur the nationality of the finished product, so that nationalistic governments will be willing to purchase it.

> . . . the idea is that an airplane that is multinational in its parts and its fabrication offers the seller political advantages in the world market. All the major suppliers and their governments see a need to dilute the national character of their products. They also know that one company cannot any longer take on the full burden of making a commercial airplane — or an engine for that matter. Any supplier who launches a new airplane program or a new engine program must involve innumerable other companies, large and small, which are spread around the major industrialized nations of the West and extend to Japan as well. A fierce competition for risk-sharing partners and subcontractors is under way.[9]

The traditional rationale for joint ventures has been that the skills of both partners are necessary to make the business venture in question a success. Either company acting alone would not succeed. Another force now seems to be creating joint ventures between the smaller companies in an industry — the need to achieve economies of scale similar to those enjoyed by their larger competitors. Thus two computer firms form a joint venture to produce peripheral equipment, reducing their aggregate research and development budget and lowering their variable production costs. Automobile manufacturers establish joint engine and transmission plants to achieve economies which neither could obtain alone. Giovanni Agnelli, chairman of Fiat, recently predicted that the component businesses of many European car makers will be combined in coming years, although separate trademarks and sales organisations will be maintained.[10] The essence of his argument is that the volume of cars produced in Europe is too small to support ten different companies, so joint ventures to achieve economies of scale are a likely solution.

One further factor underlying the formation of joint ventures may be that in recent years the public has generally been hostile to business and that governments have proved themselves to be unreliable in many ways, leading to an unwillingness on the part of firms to tackle major projects alone. It is not surprising that businessmen predict, albeit reluctantly, that they will be using more joint ventures in the years ahead.

We now turn our attention to the factors which cause managers to be such reluctant users of joint ventures.

Why Are Joint Ventures Difficult to Manage?

If one asks any manager, North American or European, which is more difficult to manage, a wholly owned subsidiary or a joint venture, the chances are high that the joint venture will get the nod. Further questioning is likely to reveal that this is not because joint ventures are given more difficult tasks to perform, but because they are a much more difficult form of organisation to manage well. Joint venture problems tend to be internal, not external.

The basic cause of the problem is that joint ventures have more than one parent. These parents, unlike the shareholders of a widely held public corporation, are visible and powerful and can and will disagree on just about anything: how fast the joint venture should grow, which products and markets it should encompass, how it should be organised and perhaps even what constitutes good or bad management. Should the venture be managed for short-term gain or long-term market-share creation?

There are two specific areas within a joint venture where the problems of multiple parents can make themselves known. One is at the board level. The board of directors of a joint venture contains representatives from each parent and it is here that differences in priorities, direction and perhaps values will emerge. The result can be confusion, frustration, possibly bitterness and a resulting slowness to take decisions. Several examples should be sufficient to illustrate the type of problems which can arise. The board of directors of one company in my study, consisting of American and British managers, continually disagreed vehemently about the amount of data required before a decision could be made. The British could not understand why the Americans wanted 'all those numbers'. The Americans, on the other hand, believed the British were totally 'flying blind'. This problem was serious, as it meant that either the Americans had to agree to proceed with what they considered to be insufficient information, or the British had to incur a delay and spend extra money collecting information which they did not feel was necessary. From this beginning, the problem became even worse. The British accused the Americans of not trusting them. At the time the venture was formed the Americans had stressed their need for the British parent's market knowledge. Now the British were using this knowledge and it was obvious that the Americans didn't trust it. Why have a joint venture, they asked, if you don't trust our judgement?

The second example involves a joint venture general manager who, I believe, was one of the most skilled that I came across in two years of travel and research. He had managed his venture for more than ten years and taken it from $4 million in sales to $60 million. His situation demonstrates the problems which a joint venture board can present to even the most experienced general manager. In this particular circumstance the venture need to build a new plant. The manager and his American board members felt that the new plant should not be located in the same European country as the existing plant since they would then both fall under the jurisdiction of the same union, making simultaneous strike action very probable. However, the European board members wanted the plant built in the same country, so that it could absorb workers which their company planned to lay off in one of its existing plants. The joint venture manager described his course of action.

The first move was to discuss the situation separately with each parent, to see how strongly each would hold to its position. I concluded that the local parent would not budge. As a result, I began a series of trips to Chicago (disguised location), which averaged *two a month, for a full year*, to negotiate with the Americans, who were supplying critical technology to the venture. I told them they really only had three options; sell out, buy the local parent out, or agree that the plant should be built in the same country as the existing one. However, at the same time, I convinced the local parent to agree to pay a grant to the venture in return for hiring its workers. Once each side saw that other was making concessions, they agreed to go along.

Even an issue as straightforward as a plant location decision can become complex and drawn out in a joint venture. In this case each parent had to be convinced that the other was not getting preferential treatment. Of course differences of opinion over an issue like plant location can arise between managers in a wholly owned subsidiary as well, but in this forum neither participant is likely to have the power to terminate the whole operation, a power which venture partners often do have. If the goodwill and skill of both partners are critical to a venture's success, then a majority partner cannot afford to run roughshod over a minority partner's wishes. Managers of several 51-49 and 60-40 ventures explained that for this reason they had to manage their ventures as if they were 50-50 ventures. Clearly an experienced manager is required to deal with a joint venture board of directors. This is no place for a rookie.

The other aspect of joint venture operation which differentiates ventures from other forms of organisation is their staffing. Many ventures use both general and functional managers drawn from their parents. In fact a few ventures use two general managers, one taken from each parent. I have read of one such venture in Japan, which failed, and encountered one in Europe in my own study. The rationale for this arrangement appears to be, purely and simply, a lack of trust in one's partner. Each manager is given the mandate both to manage the venture and look after his parent's interests. In the Japanese case each manager could spend virtually no money without the approval of the other. Not surprisingly, the working relationship between two managers in this situation tends to be strained, cumbersome and in-efficient. The European venture structured in this manner was run by a commercial director supplied by the local parent and a technical director from the foreign parent. They were to act as joint managing directors. It soon became obvious to both parents, however, that the commercial director was unsatisfactory. Furthermore, the best candidate to replace him was an employee of the foreign firm. However the local parent stated that this foreigner could be given the job only if the current technical director, supplied by the foreign parent, were removed and a local man put in to maintain the balance of power. Amazingly enough, this was done. The exercise was very delicate and time consuming, but the venture did survive.

Problems of dual parent staffing arise more frequently at the functional management level. If a joint venture has been formed to combine the technical knowledge and skills of a foreign parent with the market and financial knowledge of a local parent, the venture will often contain engineering and production managers supplied by the foreign parent and financial and marketing managers supplied by the local parent. These executives may be on loan, retaining their seniority and pension rights in the parent company, but even if they are not there is often an implicit message given to them that if they perform well they may be promoted back into the parent company. As a result functional managers may pay more attention to events taking place in their parent and to signals coming from that parent, than they do to the venture's general manager. One West Coast general manager summarised his problems of trying to create a cohesive management team from a group of executives whose attention and loyalty lay largely outside the venture:

> You have to rule by strength of will. You cannot use your organizational position; because you are not sure where the loyalties of those below you really lie. The people who work for you are not necessarily appointed by you, so your hire/fire/promotion powers are limited.

This problem reached a peak in one European joint venture shortly before it collapsed. The general manager and two functional managers had been provided by the local parent, two other functional managers came from the American parent. An executive in the US company who was on the venture's board of directors explained the situation:

> As things got tough in the market, they started to make changes in the venture which we did not approve of, and our functional managers reported them to us. The problem was that our managers were not supposed to be communicating directly with us. Our information was supposed to come from the general manager. At

a board meeting, we made the mistake of asking some very pointed questions which made it clear that we knew some things which they didn't want us to. The unfortunate result was that our manager who had given us the information was cut off by the others, and we got nothing more. Over time, the split between the managers from the two companies grew, and the place practically became an armed camp.

The general manager of this venture commented 'you can paper over the cracks and the divided loyalties in the good times, it's in the hard times that the differences in underlying allegiances really show up.'

These examples go some way toward explaining the high failure rate of joint ventures. Quite a number of studies indicate that 30-40 per cent of all joint ventures fail, some of which are summarised below.

My own study of 37 joint ventures contained seven which collapsed during the two years the study was being conducted, while five underwent major reorganisations due to poor performance. This yields an 'in trouble' rate of approximately 30 per cent.

A major Harvard study of 1100 joint ventures formed prior to 1967 between American firms and partners in other developed countries showed an instability rate of 30 per cent. As will be discussed subsequently, instability (a switch in control, a takeover by one partner, or liquidation) is not necessarily synonymous with poor performance, but it is probably related.[11]

At least 90 joint ventures collapsed in Japan between 1972 and mid-1976. These collapses followed a major boom in the creation of ventures in that country in the 1960s, although it is not known what proportion of existing ventures the 90 failures represented.

In the US study of 123 joint ventures formed since 1924 in the basic chemical industry, Thompson found that 40 or 50 per cent no longer existed as joint ventures by 1967. More than half of these had been purchased by one parent or a third party. Others failed because of obsolete facilities or products, unsuccessful research, depressed prices, and so on. Half of the ventures that did not survive lasted five years or less and over 80 per cent lasted ten years or less.[12]

Are Some Joint Ventures Easier to Manage?

Clearly, on average, joint ventures have a high failure rate. But are they all equally difficult to manage? The answer is that they are not: some are easier to manage than others and have a markedly lower failure rate as a result. The remainder of this book deals with the identification of both difficult and easier types of joint ventures, discussing when each type can be used and how to design and manage each. Particular emphasis is given to the more difficult type of venture.

In Chapter Two a fundamental question of joint venture design and management is addressed: how joint should a venture be? Obviously the ownership of a joint venture is shared, but what else should be shared? Should the venture be staffed with employees from both companies? Presumably the board will be joint, containing executives from each parent company, but what role should it play? Some boards are largely ceremonial, others are heavily involved in ongoing operations. Addressing questions like these led me to categorise joint ventures into three types; dominant parent ventures, shared management ventures and independent ventures. Chapter Three provides a detailed illustration of two joint ventures, one dominant and one shared, each being used to develop techniques to mine and process manganese nodules on the ocean floor. These comparative case studies allow a close look at the structure and management of these two types of ventures which can superficially appear similar but which in reality are different in very important ways.

In Chapters Four and Five the questions of how to design and manage a shared joint venture are addressed. Share management ventures are the most difficult type of joint venture to manage, but in some situations they are the only possible alternative. In spite of their high failure rate, such ventures can be managed successfully, and these chapters present examples of both successes and failures, identifying those practices which will maximise a venture's probability of success. Chapter Four deals with the design of shared management ventures, discussing when such ventures are really necessary and talking about choice of a partner, staffing issues and the design of a reward system for the venture's parents. The latter topic includes a close look at product flows between a venture and its parents. Chapter Five discusses the management of a shared management venture from the viewpoint of its general manager, examining issues of ambiguous relationships, allegiance, trust and autonomy.

Chapter Six stands somewhat apart from the preceding chapters of this book, at its examines joint ventures from the point of view of only one partner, the one *without* technology to bring to the venture. Nearly every piece of work on joint ventures considers the other partner's viewpoint, that of the firm with the technology. To redress this imbalance Chapter Six discusses when different types of licence agreements and joint ventures should be used by firms which want to acquire new technology.

Chapter Seven presents a pair of closely related cases in which two European firms with good technology appropriate to a developing US market form joint ventures with the same US partner, and both fail. These cases offer some very detailed insights into joint venture longevity, looking in particular at issues of partner commitment and attitude.

Chapter Eight was written six months after the others, and reflects my involvement in the establishment of new joint ventures during that period by two large multinational firms. Their calls for advice in making some difficult decisions forced me to examine in an action setting some of the principles developed in this book and gave me some further insights into the concerns of firms acting as passive parents. The chapter offers both a managerial perspective and summary of my findings and suggests areas in which further work is needed.

Notes

1. Ducker, P., *Management: Tasks, Responsibilities, Practices* (Harper and Row, New York, 1973), p. 720.

2. Schaan, J.L., 'Parent Control and Joint Ventures Success: The Case of Mexico', thesis, University of Western Ontario, forthcoming.

3. Janger, A.R., *Organization of International Joint Ventures* (The Conference Board, New York, 1980), p. 1.

4. Stopford, J.M., and Wells, L.T., *Managing the Multinational Enterprise* (Basic Books, New York, 1972).

5. LaPaslombara, J.H., and Blauk, S., *Multinational Corporations in Comparative Perspective* (The Conference Board, New York, 1977), pp. 37–8.

6. Franko, L.G., *The European Multinationals* (Harper and Row, London, 1976). See particularly Ch. 5.

7. *Mergers and Acquisitions: The Journal of Corporate Venture* (published quarterly by Information for Industry Inc., Mclean, Virginia).

8. Janger, *International Joint Ventures*, p. 1.

9. 'A Reporter At Large, A Sporty Game – 1, Betting the Company', *The New Yorker*, 14 June 1982.

10. As quoted in *Time* magazine, 9 August 1982, p. 43.

11. Franko, L.G., *Joint Venture Survival in Multinational Corporations* (Praeger Publishers, New York, 1971), pp. 3–4.

12. Thompson's data were reported by Berg, S.V., and Friedman, P., in 'Joint Ventures in American Industry' (Part One), *Mergers and Acquisitions*, vol. 13, no. 2, Summer 1978.

2 HOW JOINT SHOULD A VENTURE BE?

Are some joint ventures in fact easier to manage than others? It would certainly seem so. There are several industries in which joint ventures are used successfully in a very routine, matter of fact fashion. These ventures present no special difficulties to their managers and are simply viewed as an expedient way of doing business. This is the case in the land development and construction business, for instance, where joint ventures are commonly used to obtain sufficient financing to assemble large tracts of land or to undertake major building projects. Typically one partner will simply be a provider of funds and know little about the particular business in question. The other parent actually manages the venture. Even in joint ventures in which both companies do have the skills to play an active management role many managers believe that the venture will be more successful if one firm is willing to play a passive role. One experienced manager outlined his firm's approach to such situations:

> The partners come to a point at which they realize that a joint venture would make sense. Then they look at each other, to decide who has the skills most appropriate to manage it, and who has the most to lose if it fails. On those considerations they decide which firm will manage it – they cannot both run it. The passive firm takes a minority of the equity and stays out of the way. It takes a lot of trust to do that, but it is essential if the venture is to work.

The notion that ventures dominated by one parent will be easier to manage than those in which both parents play an active role fits well with the argument expressed earlier than the fundamental cause of managerial difficulties in joint ventures is the fact that they have more than one parent. The more a venture can be run *as if* it has only one parent, the simpler will be the management task. In my research I measured the extent to which a venture was dominated by either of its parents by focusing on the way in which decisions were made and, in particular, by determining how much influence each parent had on various types of decisions. Joint venture general managers and parent company personnel were asked to assess the relative role of each parent and the venture's general manager in each of nine decision making

15

areas. The list included such things as pricing decisions, the replacement of a functional manager, setting sales targets and altering product design or manufacturing process. Scoring the responses allowed the ventures to be sorted into three categories: ventures dominated by one parent, these to be called *dominant parent* joint ventures; those in which both parents played an active role, labelled *shared management* ventures; and *independent ventures*, in which neither parent played a strong role. The result was that four of the ventures were independent, 13 were dominant and 20 were shared.

Dominant Parent Joint Ventures

I shall begin with an example. A dominant parent joint venture was set up in Canada in the 1970s between a Canadian and an American firm. The Americans entered the venture because they did not want to go through the screening process of Canada's Foreign Investment Review Agency. The venture was to be a world-scale plant to produce a product with which the Americans had a long history. The Canadian firm knew nothing about the product, neither its technology nor its market. However, it made a capital contribution and became a 50 per cent owner of the venture. The new company was staffed entirely by the American parent and managed by them. It was understood that, although the Canadian firm would have seats on the board, the board would not play an active decision making role. Much of the venture's output was to be sold to other divisions of the US parent, and there was a provision in the joint venture agreement that the transfer price paid by the divisions would drop after the venture had earned a 30 per cent return on assets. In effect, this put a limit on the return which could be earned by the Canadian partner. However, given the world leading expertise of the US firm and the promise of a low-cost plant, the Canadians felt that it was likely that their actual return on investment would be the maximum allowed for in the joint venture provisions.

This venture is in many ways a typical dominant parent joint venture. The important feature of dominant parent joint ventures is that they are managed by their dominant parents virtually as if they were wholly owned subsidiaries. The board of directors, although containing executives from each parent, plays a largely ceremonial role. All of the ventures' operating and strategic decisions are made by dominant parent executives, located either in the joint venture or

Figure 2.1: The Dominant Parent Joint Venture

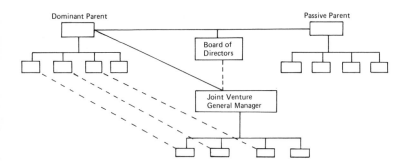

the parent company. As diagrammed above, the general manager of a dominant parent venture, while nominally acting as the chief executive officer of an independent company, will in fact report to an executive of the dominant parent company, typically a senior product group manager or a manager responsible for international operations. The venture manager may be granted more or less autonomy to run his own show, but this will be decided by the manager to whom he reports, not the board. All of the functional managers in the joint venture (production, finance, marketing, engineering, etc.) will come from or be selected by the dominant parent. None will come from the passive parent. These men too will often have a reporting relationship to a superior in the parent company, as well as the more formal link to the joint venture general manager. In terms of job evaluation, both the general and functional managers are likely to be assessed *vis-à-vis* other division and subsidiary managers. The joint venture is integrated into the dominant parent's management system, just as if it were a wholly owned subsidiary.

The scoring system which was used to sort ventures into the dominant and shared categories yielded results which fell on a continuum between ventures totally dominated by one parent at one extreme, and those absolutely equally shared at the other. The actual dividing point which I used (after taking out the independents) was at a natural break in the continuum, between these two extremes. This means that some ventures in the dominant parent category are somewhat less dominated by a single parent than others just as some of the shared management ventures are not as equally shared as others.

In the interest of completeness a description is given below of a dominant parent venture which was slightly less controlled by its dominant parent than the case described earlier.

This second venture was in England, and its parents were American and British. The venture operated in a line of business familiar to both parents, although it was completely staffed by the British parent. In fact the joint venture manager was still on the British parent's payroll and was managing the joint venture on a part-time basis. Since it was a 50-50 venture the Americans held half of the seats on the board, and they wanted the board to become much more active in decision making. As one US executive commented, 'We spent a lot of time working out the accounting and legal ramifications of this venture, but virtually no time deciding how it would be managed.' In the result, the venture was dominated by the British, although the Americans had made a few inroads. The Americans believed that one of their problems was their physical distance from the venture. The executives explained: 'Communication was part of the problem. The British would work things out amongst themselves on the phone or in informal meetings. By the time we got something in writing in New York, the decision had been made, their position hardened.' In spite of the American frustration, the venture was performing very well.

The primary difference between these two dominant parent ventures appear to be in the degree of willingness which one partner demonstrated to play a passive role. In fact the American push for participation in the British venture may have been entirely misguided. As statistics to be presented subsequently show, dominant parent ventures have a much better success rate than shared management ventures, the latter being what the Americans wanted in Britain. It can be difficult, of course, for a potentially dominant parent firm to find a partner willing to play a passive role. The passive partner which may be supplying large sums of money or important technology to a venture over which it will exert very little influence, needs to have a great deal of trust in the competence and honesty of the dominant parent. Although both parents will be given seats on the board of directors, this body is likely to meet seldom and in a rather perfunctory fashion.

Another aspect of dominance that these two ventures demonstrate is that dominance and ownership are not necessarily related. A firm can dominate a venture without having a dominant ownership position; both of these dominant parent ventures were 50-50 deals. Similarly, as the figures below show, the management of a venture can be shared even when the parents do not have equal ownership positions.

Table 2.1: Ownership and Dominance

Ownership	Dominant Parent	Shared Management	Independent
50–50[a]	4	15	4
51–49	3	–	–
Other	6	5	
Total	13	20	4

Note: a. 50–50 includes any equally owned venture e.g. 33–33–33, etc.

Shared Management Ventures

Once again, it may be best to start with an example. In 1975 a shared management venture was formed in the Eastern United States between a US multinational firm and a large successful German company. The German firm wanted to find a way to enter the US market, and the American company wanted to secure a viable future for a small division which was in the same business as the German company, but not performing particularly well. The Americans contributed the division's physical assets, people, and a small US market share to the venture, and the Germans added what was considered to be the best technology in the world for the product in question. The ownership of the venture was split 50-50. The venture's general manager was provided by the US company, as were most of the functional managers, although the Germans supplied both a senior and a junior technical man. The general manager reported to an executive committee which consisted of one executive from each parent company. Both parents had a high degree of influence on decisions made by the joint venture, but in a very different fashion. The Germans were in touch with venture personnel every day, primarily in relation to technical issues but also with respect to marketing techniques. Executives in the German company estimated that in total three to five telexes were being sent from the parent to the venture every day, along with a longer letter, plus two or three phone calls per week. In addition several weeks were spent each year training venture personnel in Germany, and for several more weeks per year very specialised German personnel were sent to the joint venture to further train the Americans. In spite of this high degree of interaction, when it came to determining the future direction of the venture the Germans told the general manager 'whatever you want to do is O.K. with us, just go ahead'. In practice of course, the Germans significantly shaped the venture's activities through their constant presence. The general manager of the venture described it as a 'father-daughter' relationship in which the Germans were very protective of his young company.

The American involvement, on the other hand, was much more formal, with very strict control and accounting procedures to be followed and a strong emphasis on short-term performance. Any decision of consequence in the venture had to be approved by the top management and even the board of directors of the American multi-national. It was clear to the venture's general manager that he was being evaluated on two very different sets of criteria by his two parents, and his personal strategy was to aim at the highest standard set for each criterion, thus pleasing both parents. In spite of the fact that the venture had been performing very well, he saw difficult times ahead. He believed that the Germans, because of their expertise in the product's ever-changing technology, would gradually take a larger role in the venture, and he sensed that the Americans would have to back away from their decision-making role if the venture was to remain successful. He was not sure if or how the Americans would be able to do this.

This example shows how, in a shared management venture, both parents play a meaningful managerial role. The mechanisms by which they do this can vary, and devices for controlling a joint venture are discussed in detail later in the chapter. In the example just related, the venture's general manager formally reported to an executive committee of the board six or seven times per year. In fact, he met with each of the two men on the committee, separately, much more often than that. This general manager, as did a number of others in this study, dealt with his two parents separately as much as possible, bringing them together only when it was absolutely necessary. In comparison with a dominant parent venture, it is clear that shared management ventures are much more likely to have a board or executive committee that has real influence, and it is also more likely to have functional managers drawn from both parents. Twelve of the twenty shared management ventures in this study had functional managers from each parent, and in several of those that did not, it was only because the venture was too small to justify full-time managers. Only two of the thirteen dominant parent ventures contained managers from passive parents, and in both cases this appeared to be a mistake. A typical shared management venture is diagrammed below, showing the links between the functional managers and their parent companies, with the general manager reporting to the board rather than to one of the parents.

Figure 2.2: The Shared Management Joint Venture

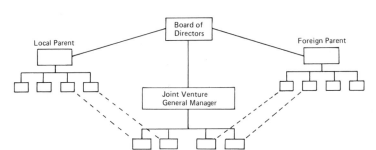

Two further points should be made. As could be seen in the German-American venture described earlier, the parents' need for each other (or more precisely the joint venture's need for each of its parents) may change over time. Nineteen parent companies responded to a question concerning the extent of their need for their partner. Thirteen of the nineteen indicated that at the time the venture was formed they definitely could not have operated the business in question alone. However, this was true for only six of the nineteen at the time this study was done. Eleven felt they could operate the venture at least as well as it was being run with the partner (in some cases this was not saying a lot) and the remaining two felt that, although they could operate the venture without their partner, it would not perform as well. Clearly the learning which takes place over time reduces the parents' need for one another and weakens the ties which hold the venture together. The managerial implications of this fact will be discussed in the chapter dealing with the management of shared management ventures.

The final issue relates to ownership. The point was made earlier that a venture does not need to be equally owned by its parents to have shared management. In fact one experienced and successful general manager stated that any shared management venture needed to be managed as if it were owned 50-50, regardless of the actual ownership split. His argument was that in any joint venture which depended on the goodwill and co-operation of both parents for its success the majority owner cannot 'force' issues by taking them to a vote. 'You can only do something like that once,' he stated, 'the second time you try and force it you'll lose your joint venture.'

In this manager's venture the eight-man board consisted of four executives from the American parent, three from the European parent, and himself. He had formerly been an employee of the European company. He told both parents very clearly that should any issue come to a vote at the board of directors *he would vote with the European parent executive, even if he disagreed with them*, thus creating a four-four deadlock. His message seemed to be directed at the American parent, essentially saying that he would take their side against the local parent, so all issues would have to be settled by negotiation. In 14 years of his management, no issue had ever been put to the board for a formal vote.

Independent Ventures

Only four firms fell into the independent category, so it is dangerous to make much in the way of generalisations concerning them. In order to qualify for inclusion in this group a venture's general manager had to have the freedom to make decisions on his own in six or more of the nine listed areas of decision making. It was probably not a coincidence that none of the four ventures in this category was a failure. Autonomy for a joint venture general manager seems both to be the result of success ('I'm doing all right so leave me alone') and to strengthen the possibility of further success. A more complete discussion of autonomy and statistics which show that there is a very strong relationship between the success of a joint venture and the autonomy of its general manager will be presented in Chapter Five.

Performance

All of the arguments presented thus far have pointed to the same conclusion: dominant parent ventures should outperform shared management ventures. The figures presented below suggest that this is indeed the case. Two separate performance measures were used, one being the manager's own perception of his venture's performance, the other, possibly more objective, was my own measure. I measured failure of a venture as being either its demise through liquidation (this would include one partner's taking over the venture if this was due to poor performance of the venture) or its undergoing a major reorganisation (new product line, new executives) because of poor performance. As can be seen, both measures gave the same result. Dominant parent ventures significantly outperform shared management ventures.

Table 2.2: Joint Venture Performance

| Type | | Management's Assessment | | | |
	Poor	Satis-factory	Good	Liquidated or Reorganised	Number of Ventures
Dominant Parent	23%	23%	54%	15%	13
Shared Management	55%	20%	25%	50%	20
Independent	25%	0	75%	0	4
Total	36%	22%	42%	31%	37

Although these performance measures are quite crude, the size of the difference they reveal leaves little doubt that the performance differential between the two types of venture is real. By the managers' own judgement, 77 per cent of dominant parent ventures were performing satisfactorily or better, whereas this was true for only 45 per cent of the shared management ventures. (These were 'pre-demise' readings in the case of ventures which did not survive.) A full 50 per cent of the shared management ventures were liquidated or reorganised due to poor performance, against only 15 per cent for dominant parent ventures. Taking this analysis one step further, the shared management category was subdivided further according to the balance of influence between the venture parents. As was stated earlier the range from dominant parent to shared management venture is a continuum, and the management of some shared management ventures is more equally split than that of others. The figures in Table 2.3 further support the notion that the more equally the parents share the management of a venture, the worse it will perform.

Table 2.3: Shared Management Ventures

Balance between Parents	Liquidated or Reorganised	Number of Ventures
Equal	62.5%	8
Slight Imbalance	50%	8
Larger Imbalance[a]	25%	4

Note: a. In these ventures the stronger parent is still less dominant than the strong parent in a dominant parent joint venture.

In order to place firms into these categories I have, in effect, measured the 'bottom line', that is, how much influence each parent has on various types of decisions affecting the venture. The ways in which parent companies can obtain such influence are many and varied and range from being very direct to quite subtle. The remainder of this chapter illustrates the ways in which firms influence joint ventures. It draws heavily on the work of Jean-Louis Schaan, a doctoral student who, under my guidance, has been examining the operation of joint ventures in Mexico.[1]

Techniques of Joint Venture Control

Schaan chose to study joint ventures operating in Mexico because it is a country in which a foreign firm cannot hold a majority ownership position in a joint venture. He wondered if it still made sense for foreign multinationals to form ventures in Mexico. In trying to answer this question, Schaan investigated the relationship between control and success. As a part of the study, he has examined the various ways in which Mexican and foreign parents have exercised control over their ventures. He discovered that parent companies use a much greater variety of mechanisms to influence the management of joint ventures than has generally been recognised. These will be discussed under three headings: formal agreements, staffing and influence techniques.

Formal Agreements

There are a variety of legal documents which invariably accompany the creation of a joint venture. These are nearly always closely connected to the issue of control. The articles of incorporation, by-laws and shareholders' agreements, which are in a legal sense the cornerstone of any venture, spell out such things as the scope of the venture, the composition of the board and the executive committee, the type of decisions which need to come to the board for approval and the percentage of votes needed to approve various types of decision. There is very often protection built in for the minority shareholder on certain issues. These documents deal directly with control in its most direct form: who can veto what?

In addition to these basic agreements, there is very often a series of agreements between the joint venture and the foreign partner. These could cover the supply of component parts, possibly the marketing of the venture's products in countries beyond that in which it is located and the supply of product design and production process technology. When such deals are struck, management's attention is often focused on royalty fees and transfer prices. However, in a more subtle way, each of these agreements confers some degree of control to the foreign partner. If, for instance, the venture can obtain its technology from no other source, the foreign parent will effectively control the product design, much of the economics of the production process, the rate of introduction of product modifications, and so on. Similarly through the supply of component parts the foreign parent will automatically be involved in questions of production scheduling, modification of the product for the local market, and whether or not to build products for inventory. A marketing agreement will obviously give control over export volumes and involve the parent in discussions of pricing, advertising, distribution and product features. The more the parent is involved in such discussions on an ongoing basis, the greater its influence.

Agreements with the local parent are less often for technology and more often for local services such as legal work, accounting and computer time. In addition, all of the venture's output may be sold to the local partner for resale in the local market. In some cases a management contract may be signed, giving the local parent explicit control over day-to-day operations. Although such a contract often places the recipient firmly in a position of dominance, this is not necessarily the case. The information in Table 2.4 indicates the proportion of firms in my sample of 37 ventures using each of these pay-off/control techniques. The suitability of each of these pay-off techniques is further discussed in Chapter Four.

Table 2.4: Pay-off and Control Mechanisms

	Percentage of Parent Firms Using Each Mechanism					
	Management Fee	Technical Fee	Dividend	Goods Sold to Venture	Goods Purchased From Venture	Tech. Used As Initial Equity
Dominant Parent Ventures						
Dominant Parents	25%	25%	31%	15%	15%	33%
Passive Parents	0%	15%	31%	31%	23%	33%
Shared Management Ventures						
Local Parents	28%	11%	35%	20%	30%	33%
Foreign Parents	16%	58%	35%	55%	15%	37%

In a joint venture of any complexity these agreements which simultaneously give pay-offs and varying amounts of control can proliferate quickly. Negotiating them is a major task and managing a venture which has many such agreements is very difficult, because a change in the venture's operations will have an impact on many of these areas. Before approving any change each parent will do a detailed analysis of its gains and losses against those of the other parent if the change is implemented. One manager particularly afflicted with this problem ran a venture which bought components from each parent, made use of administrative services and leased office and warehouse space from the American parent, used engineering work provided by the German parent and sales leads from the American parent. The monetary benefits flowing to each parent are listed in Table 2.5.

Table 2.5: Sources of Parent Pay-off and Control in Baker–Amcoal Joint Venture[a]

To Baker Gmbh	To American Coal Corporation
1. 50% of all dividends	1. 50% of all dividends
2. an engineering fee based on joint venture selling prices:	2. 3% of cost of goods sold in recompense for sales leads
(a) 7% if Baker had to perform prototype design and testing	3. a warehousing fee, to compensate Amcoal for the space taken in its warehouses by venture parts
(b) 5% if some engineering was required, but no testing	4. an administrative fee in return for administrative services performed for the joint venture
(c) 3% if no engineering was required	5. coverage of overheads in addition to variable cost on parts manufactured for the joint venture
3. coverage of overheads in addition to variable cost on parts manufactured for the joint venture	

Note: a. Disguised name.

More detail is provided on this venture, and its general manager, in Chapters Five and Seven. The point to be made at this juncture is that each additional complexity of this agreement, while possibly increasing control for the parents, also makes the general manager's job more difficult.

Staffing

Arrangements regarding a joint venture's staffing are generally not quite as formal as the agreements just discussed. From a control point of view, however, they can be very important. There are several immediate advantages to a parent interested in controlling a venture in having its personnel in the venture. Communication between the venture and the parent company is likely to be improved, simply because employees of the two firms will know each other. More complete information offers the prospect of more complete control.

Secondly, such an employee is likely to act in ways which his parent would find acceptable, even when his actions are not being overtly controlled. His values and attitudes will most probably have been shaped by the parent company and will continue to guide him even in the joint venture. Schaan found several other techniques being used to ensure the continuing loyalty of joint venture personnel.

1. In two of the ten Mexican joint ventures the general manager remained on the parent's payroll.
2. In four ventures the general manager's bonus was tied to one parent's results.
3. In four ventures the general manager was required to attend the parent's world-wide management or technical meetings.
4. In five ventures the promotion and career plans of the general manager were clearly predicated upon his returning to the parent company.

There is no evidence to suggest that these practices lead to more successful joint ventures. To the extent that they contribute to the dominance of a venture by one parent, they may well do so. However, in shared management ventures such activities prevent the venture from developing its own identity, separate from that of the parents. This may hinder successful operation of the venture. This subject is discussed further in Chapter Five.

Influence Techniques

Schaan found that some parent companies were able to influence significantly the thinking of joint venture executives even in situations in which they had no formal means of control. For example, in five instances parents asked the ventures to use appropriation request forms which they had designed. By specifying the kind of information and amount of detail to be provided, these parents felt they could influence the kind of projects submitted by the venture and the kind of returns they would strive for. Some parents also used 'strategy reviews' or progress reports with the same intent. Taking this process one step further were the companies who loaned staff personnel to the venture to assist with planning and to do some in-house training. At least one general manager complained that this process was going too far, stating that the staff services provided by the local parent were for its benefit, not the joint venture's.

Some firms found that using a former joint venture manager as the executive to whom the current venture manager had to report was very effective. Because the experienced manager could offer many insights into the operation of the venture to the current manager, he was able to exert a great deal of influence. Less subtle was the relationship in four ventures in which the venture clearly reported to one parent in advance of the other. Schaan quoted one general manager as follows:

> Before I present any project to the Mexican parent, I need the non-objection of my boss, who is the president for the Mexican operations of the American parent, and the executive committee and the board in the US.

Reviewing his extensive evidence on techniques of controlling joint ventures, Schaan concluded that there were two quite different types of control being exercised. 'Positive control' was the label he gave to techniques by which a parent could lead or encourage a venture in a certain direction. These were primarily the staffing and the influence techniques just discussed. 'Negative control' he defined as the ability to stop the venture from doing something. Negative control most often rested in the formal agreements described in the section on Formal Agreements. Positive control appears to be an ongoing process of influence, whereas negative control is more an exercise of raw power, which should not have to be employed if positive control mechanisms are in place and being used properly.

After considering both Schaan's work and my own, I would conclude that parent firms with no previous joint venture experience are likely to concentrate much too heavily on the negative aspects of control. It takes time and experience to learn some of the subtle techniques which make up positive control. For this reason inexperienced firms may be more likely to avoid minority ownership positions. However, as the latter portion of the chapter has shown, the link between ownership and control is very tenuous; a minority ownership position does not necessarily imply a position of weak control.

Summary

The overwhelming fact presented in this chapter is that shared management joint ventures have a dramatically higher failure rate than dominant parent ventures. I have argued that this is because shared management ventures are more difficult to manage. The other possible explanation is that shared management ventures have a higher failure rate because they are used to take on exceptionally difficult tasks, tasks in which any joint venture would fail. I do not believe this to be the case, and in the next chapter I have documented the development of two joint ventures used to tackle the identical task, the development of a system of mining the seabed. It would have been ideal for my argument if the shared management venture had failed while the dominant parent survived, but in the undersea mining business nothing is so clear-cut. Both ventures achieved their limited technical goals but neither achieved, for political reasons the major long-term goal of creating a producing mine. Nevertheless the parallel study of these two ventures presents a revealing comparison of the two forms of joint venture, showing the advantages and disadvantages of each.

Notes

1. Schaan, J.L., 'Parent Control and Joint Venture Success: The Case of Mexico', thesis, University of Western Ontario, forthcoming.

3 COMPARATIVE CASE STUDIES: DOMINANT AND SHARED VENTURES ON THE SEABED

This chapter examines the formation and management of two joint ventures created to develop techniques to mine and process manganese nodules lying on the floor of the Pacific Ocean, three miles beneath the surface. One participant likened the task to 'hanging a long straw off the top of the Empire State Building to suck BBs off the sidewalk.' In spite of the difficult of the task, five international joint ventures had been formed by 1980, attracted by the nickel, copper, cobalt, molybdenum and manganese contained in between 90 billion and 1,700 billion tons of nodules (an imprecision typical of undersea mining estimates) lying on the ocean floor. The value of the minerals contained in a ton of seabed nodules was estimated as high as $100, compared with a value of perhaps $10 per ton of ore in land-based copper mines.

The companies involved in the five joint ventures were based in the United States, Canada, the United Kingdom, Japan, Germany, France, Belgium, Italy and Holland. Many, like Inco and Kennecott, were long-established mining companies already mining and processing the same minerals on land as would be extracted from the nodules. Other firms, like Lockheed of California and Sedco of Texas, saw undersea mining as a diversification with outstanding growth potential. Lockheed had extensive experience building equipment to operate in hostile environments as part of the US space programme and reasoned that its expertise could be useful in building systems to operate on the seabed. Sedco, although a fraction of the size of the other companies involved in undersea mining, was one of the world's largest international marine drilling contractors and saw the development of undersea mining systems as a natural extension of its skills. Other firms, particularly in Japan, were looking for access to long-term sources of mineral supply. Although a number of companies had started investigating undersea mining on their own in the 1960s, by 1980 all of them had formed joint ventures as the complexity and magnitude of the task became clearer.

Although the five joint ventures were formed to accomplish the same objective, namely developing and then operating a workable undersea mining system, there were significant differences among them.

30

Table 3.1: Undersea-Mining Participants[a]

Joint Venture	Country	Stake	Year Formed	Mining Technology	Processing Technology
1. Ocean Mining Associates[b]					
U.S. Steel	U.S.	33 1/3		Dredge device with air lift	Hydrochloric acid leach
Union Miniere	Belgium	33 1/3			
Sun Co.	U.S.	33 1/3			
2. Ocean Management Inc.					
Inco	Canada	25	1975	Dredge device with hydraulic or air lift	Pyrometallurgical
Sedco	U.S.	25			
Preussag	West Germany	25			
Metallgesellschaft	West Germany				
Salzgitter	West Germany				
Domco (led by Sumitomo)	Japan	25			
3. Ocean Minerals[a]					
Lockheed	U.S.	30	1978	Dredge device with with hydraulic or air lift	Unspecified
Amoco	U.S.	30			
Shell	Britain/Holland	30			
Bos Kalis Westminster	Holland	10			
4. Kennecott					
Kennecott Copper	U.S.	50	1973	Dredge device with hydraulic lift	Ammonia leach
Noranda	Canada	10			
Consolidated Gold Fields	Britain	10			
Rio Tinto-Zinc	Britain	10			
BP	Britain	10			
Mitsubishi	Japan	10			
5. Afernod[c]					
Center National Pour L'Exploitation des Oceans	France			Unspecified studying dredge and continuous line bucket	Unspecified
Commissariat a L'Energie Atomique	France				
Bureau de Recherches Geologiques et Minieres	France				
Le Nickel	France				
France-Dunkirk	France				

Notes: a. As of 1980. b. ENI of Italy later joined this group, giving each firm a 25% share. c. Participation percentages are not publicly available; the figures for Ocean Minerals are estimates based on hearsay.
Source: (except for formation date) Report by H. Emzer, US Department of the Interior, as quoted in *The Economist*, 31 May, 1980.

As shown in Table 3.1, the smallest number of participants in any venture was three and the largest, six. (However, Domco, a member of Ocean Management Incorporated (OMI), was in fact owned by 23 Japanese firms.) Afernod of France was the only venture made up of firms from a single country, although all of the British companies belonged to the same venture and tended to act in concert. OMI and the Kennecott venture had the widest international participation. All of the ventures except Kennecott's were owned equally by their parents, an external indication of Kennecott's desire to establish a dominant parent joint venture.

Executives interviewed throughout this study were concerned about the degree to which one partner could and should dominate a venture and this issue receives particular attention in this chapter. What, exactly, are the pros and cons of using dominant parent and shared management ventures, when the business task at hand is extremely complex? The chapter begins with a discussion of the task taken on by these joint ventures and the way in which this task changed over time.

The Nature of the Task

Reviewing the brief history of man's efforts to mine the oceans, the president of one joint venture commented how much easier everything had seemed in the early years. Although the technology of undersea mining was then underdeveloped and the relative economics of mining the sea versus conventional mining were nothing but guesses, these were problems the firms felt competent to tackle. The factor which changed the situation dramatically between 1970 and 1980 was the introduction of political and legal uncertainties, crystallised in the negotiations taking place at the Law of the Sea Conferences. The basic question of who owned the minerals on the seabed was quickly transformed into a set of much more pointed questions: Who would grant permits to the mining companies allowing them access to certain mine sites? Who would tax their earnings? Would their production rate be controlled? If the seabed was the common heritage of mankind, how were the interests of developing countries, with no technology to mine the seabed themselves, to be protected? Although the mining firms became involved in the Law of the Sea Conference which debated these issues, most executives felt quite powerless to influence the outcome or even to predict what it might be.

By 1980 no Law of the Sea Treaty had been signed, although the mining companies were extremely concerned that the US government, which played a major role in the conference's seven sessions, might be preparing to agree to some very unpalatable treaty provisions. The draft text of the treaty proposed in 1978 called for the establishment of an International Seabed Authority which would create an Enterprise to mine the seabed in competition with private firms. This Authority would be a body in which each country had one vote, and consequently it would be effectively controlled by Third World countries The private companies did not object to this concept as long as the Enterprise's competition was 'fair'. But other provisions of the draft treaty seemed to insure that this would not be the case. The treaty called for forced technology transfer from all private mining companies to the Enterprise, as well as the cession to the Enterprise of one prospected mine site for each mine site actually developed by a mining company. Other provisions were designed to restrict production output for 25 years and to keep prices high, in each case to protect the interests of land-based producers.

In view of the limited progress made by the 156-nation Law of the Sea Conference, a number of US legislators, with the whole-hearted support of most mining companies (with the notable exception of Inco), were pressing the US Congress to enact domestic legislation which would insure the mining companies against retroactive losses of equipment and facilities, should they start operation before the finalisation of a Law of the Sea Treaty and subsequently be penalised by it. The US State Department was concerned that such a move would destroy the Law of Sea Conference. But a similar unilateral action with respect to 200-mile fishing limits had been successful and, in spite of dire predictions, the Conference had survived. Mining industry officials were much more optimistic about the legislation's being enacted than about a Law of the Sea Treaty's ever being ratified. They hoped to see domestic legislation in force by 1980 or 1981.

While the political and legal uncertainties facing the joint ventures increased with the passing of time, some technical and economic questions were being resolved. To mine manganese nodules successfully a firm first has to find them, then devise a method of raising them to the surface, transferring them to shore and processing them most efficiently to recover the desired minerals. Although potato-sized manganese nodules are strewn over much of the Pacific Ocean floor, just finding them is not enough. A good mine site will be not only densely strewn with nodules, but also benign -- that is, it will contain few pot-holes or underwater cliffs which could trap or overturn a mining unit. The companies looked for 20-year mine sites. To exhaust 50 per cent of a mine site after 20 years at one million tons per year would require a 2,500-square-mile site with a concentration of one pound of nodules per square foot. In view of the political situation described earlier and the fact that no full-scale mining systems had yet been developed, a venture finding a suitable site was faced with a dilemma: either to make publicly an unenforceable claim or to keep the site secret and risk its being discovered by someone else. Some firms were secretive, to the point of not informing their joint venture partners of the exact location. On the other hand, in 1973, one firm publicly informed the US government of its intention to stake a claim to a 20,000-square-mile area of the Pacific Ocean floor, giving the exact location and asking for the government's protection. No response was forthcoming.

Although the search for better mine sites could be never-ending, most firms believed that they had found at least one potentially suitable site during the 1970s. However, not all the firms were confident that they had devised appropriate systems with which to mine the sites. Four of the joint ventures were developing similar vacuum-cleaner-like devices to scoop the nodules off the seabed which were coupled to an air lift or a hydraulic lift to raise the nodules to a mining ship on the surface. Three of the five ventures held successful sea trials during the 1970s in which nodules were raised from the ocean floor, using equipment one-fifth to one-quarter the size planned for commercial use. Kennecott executives argued that small-scale tests, while adequate for developing basic technical concepts, were not useful for developing operational techniques. Since these techniques would be critically important in determining final costs of operating the system such costs could not be predicted with any accuracy until full-scale tests were carried out. Full-scale tests were expensive, however. A mining ship was estimated to cost $100 million, plus $15 million a month to operate. A full-scale test of mining equipment would cost approximately $200 million.

It is unusual to find recorded conversations of executives discussing the technical uncertainties facing them in a project. Even less frequent is the case when a number of firms are trying to solve the same problem. For this reason, excerpts from a conversation involving Mr Marne Dubs, Director of the Ocean Resources Department of Kennecott; Mr Alfred Statham, a Vice President of Inco; and Mr Philip Hawkins, a Vice President of US Steel are reproduced below. The firms clearly had different approaches to some of the technical problems they faced, and they did not agree on which problems would be the most difficult to solve. These men were speaking before the United States House of Representatives Subcommittee on International Organizations on 29 January, 1978. Mr Fraser was presiding.

Mr Fraser If all the preliminary testing and prototype operations were completed, when would you actually begin commercial operation?

Mr Hawkins Our most optimistic plans would see us in production in 1985. However, you might immediately ask what is our need to have domestic legislation, or to know the political climate under which we can operate at that time. The answer to that is we are up against a 'gate'. We have various gates we have to go through here. The next one is the building of the pilot processing plant. We figure about $50 million is involved in the construction and operation of that pilot plant. So, before we take the next step, we want to see a political climate with which we feel we could live.

Mr Fraser Where are you now with respect to a recovery means?

Mr Hawkins We have a process that has been licensed to us by a subsidiary of one of our participants in our consortium. It is a process that is being used by the Hoboken people in Belgium for presently separating out the minerals in the Zaire copper ore.

We are very satisfied with the process and think that it will work our very well, but we only have used it on a very small scale, laboratory scale, and we would not want to go ahead with the opening of a plant before we had a pilot plant.

The forms in which the metals would be separated out would be different from those that industry is currently used to and there will be a period of penetration, of customer penetration, which will be required to get them used to these new forms of the metal.

Mr Fraser I was interested also in how far along you are in the means of bringing the nodules to the surface.

Mr Hawkins We have a ship which will sail on Sunday from San Diego and will go out to the mine site that we have explored. We hope within the next month or so that we will have successfully raised 10,000 tons of nodules.

We go to bed praying every night.

Mr Fraser Is this a ship that is of sufficient capability that you would use it for commercial recovery?

Mr Hawkins No, it is a 20,000-ton ore carrier that belonged to

United States Steel. We converted it, to put a hold in the middle. We have three miles of pipe on the deck that you stick down through the hold and then you have a dredgehead that you drag along the bottom, and hope that everything comes up that you want to come up and that things that you do not want to come up do not come up . . .

We have already done it successfully 1 mile down on the Blake Plateau, but this is 3 miles down. Unfortunately, the nodules that are richest in minerals are at the greater depths.

Mr Fraser The minerals will be loaded onto the carrier itself?

Mr Hawkins Well, when we have a commercial operation, we will plan to have one carrier that will come alongside the mining ship. This one has a storage capacity of about 10,000 tons and the commercial vessel would probably be about 5 times that.

Mr Fraser Mr Dubs?

Mr Dubs Putting a commercial plant in operation before 1986 may require as much as a five-year leadtime . . . Considering just the problems of getting the site located, getting construction done, and being able to go into production, that is really the earliest that one can do it . . . Roughly half of the investment in the amount we have talked about is going to be in the onshore processing plant.

Mr Fraser Where do you expect to build . . . the processing plant?

Mr Dubs Probably on the West Coast. I am using the usual caution in giving you an approximate answer because the decision has not been made.

Mr Fraser Where are you with respect to bringing the nodules to the surface?

Mr Dubs Four years ago, we successfully tested at sea the bottom mining unit . . . In that test, we did not bring the nodules to the surface. We have tested means to do this on land and we are satisfied now that we have worked out the technology. It is our plan, which differs somewhat from that described by Mr Hawkins, to produce what we have termed a prototype ship that is essentially a commercial scale ship that would be proven out at sea for its operating characteristics.

That decision is a very expensive decision and would certainly cost in excess of $100 million . . .

Mr Fraser Mr Statham.

Mr Statham First, with respect to when we see the first commercial mining of the deep seabed to begin . . . 1985, 1986 would be the earliest . . . We think it will be substantially beyond that before market conditions are such that there is really an attractive economic investment to be made.

We engaged in 1975 a four-year feasibility study to continue our exploration efforts, to design and construct a mining test vessel, to conduct nodule processing tests and to study all of the economics.

Our ship will go to sea within the next two weeks to begin mining tests. I think that it is important to understand that there has not yet been the kind of deep sea tests that everybody would agree, I think, are essential if we are to be able to understand the economics of ocean mining. The importance of these tests can be realised if you remember that we are talking about picking up nodules 15,000 feet below the surface of the ocean and that is to be done essentially by stringing almost three miles of oil-well drilling pipe with a collector at the end to pick up nodules the size of a potato or a baseball.

We have confidence in the design of that system; we think that it will work, but we sure do not know what the efficiency of the recovery will be, either in terms of actually bringing the nodules up through that collector system or how adequately you can cover the mine site without either missing vast sections of it or with wasteful overlaps.

So, we think a lot more work has to be done before we will be able to determine what the operating cost of an ocean-mining venture will be.

With respect to processing tests, we expect to bring back 4,000 or 5,000 tons of nodules from this mining effort and process them in existing facilities in Canada and Japan. We do not foresee any major problems in processing. It is essentially an application of fairly well-known technology.

Mr Fraser Mr Dubs, you say the decision to go ahead with the ship is one of the major investments, yet apparently their companies have made it without the legislation.

Mr Dubs We have to look at it as a matter of scale. I cannot speak for them, but if I make an error, they can correct me.

My understanding of the scale of their test ship is that it is on the order of 1,000 to 1,200 tons of nodules. As we have seen the problem, it is not one of determining whether it is technically possible to mine the nodules and raise them. We think our own work, done on a somewhat different basis, has already proved that. The thing that we think has to be proven, then, is the operability on a very large scale of equipment in a reliable way so that we know what its availability will be. If the mining equipment will only operate 30 days a year, it is a different situation than when you can operate 250 days a year.

So that we think that is a crucial technical problem. We do not see how to get at that in a very small-scale test, so we have made a decision not to go through with that test.

This simply shows the diversity of the company. We could be quite wrong, but none the less, that is the decision that we have made.

It is clear from this conversation that these executives were functioning under conditions of great uncertainty; technical uncertainty, as well as political and economic. They even disagreed as to whether or not tests carried out with one-quarter scale equipment were meaningful. In addition, some executives felt that their 1980 estimates of the final cost of a ton of processed metal would be within 30 per cent of the actual cost, while others felt the error might be 100 per cent. This cost would depend on such unknown factors as the number of tons to be produced per day, the average time between equipment failures and the average down time for routine maintenance. The economic uncertainties surrounding the project were in large part tied to the price of nickel, and the comparative costs of undersea mining versus conventional onshore nickel mines. It was widely believed that undersea mining would not be cost-competitive with existing sulphide mines like Inco's in Sudbury, but might be competitive with the newer lateritic mines, particularly those to be established in the 1980s. However, a large part of the cost of new mines would be creating an infrastructure — towns, roads, hospitals, schools, airports — and it was very difficult to forecast what share of such expense the mining companies would have to pay. In short, as of 1980, no one was quite sure at what point undersea mining would produce lower-cost minerals than new onshore sources. Inco, probably the company which could forecast land-based nickel costs the most precisely, felt that undersea minerals might be competitive only sometime after 1985, barring any massive government subsidies to encourage undersea mining.

A second feature of the task facing the joint venture was the wide variety of skills required to develop the necessary hardware and operating systems. The metallurgical knowledge needed to develop a processing system for the nodules was quite distinct from the sophisticated ship-handling systems required to hold a ship on station whatever the weather, as were the skills needed to devise a nodule collector smart enough to pick up nodules rather than clay, to traverse gradients without falling off cliffs — all the while operating in a hostile environment several miles from the nearest human.

A third significant factor affecting the ventures was the fact that the outcome of the debate on the issues involved in undersea mining was of great concern to a very large number of people beyond the direct participants in the joint ventures. The major mineral-consuming countries, such as the US, Japan and West Germany, had a great deal at stake in terms of their future balance of payments and possibly national security. The countries which currently supplied these minerals, such as Canada, Chile, Zambia, Zaire, South Africa, Gabon and Brazil, potentially had a lot to lose in terms of both jobs and exports. Other countries of the Third World, neither producers nor consumers of the minerals involved, saw a chance to redress slightly the lopsided division of wealth in the world. If the seabed belonged to all of mankind, they asked, why should it be exploited only by the rich, for the benefit of the rich?

Creating the Joint Ventures

Kennecott

In 1969, Kennecott hired Marne Dubs, the first project manager of the company's ocean-mining operations. Work was proceeding in three or four different places within the company in a rather fragmented and unco-ordinated fashion and Dubs' job was to give the activities coherence and direction. Although he reported to a Vice-President, he was well aware that Kennecott's President took a strong personal interest in the company's progress in ocean mining.

In hiring a project manager for its ocean-mining operations, Kennecott was acknowledging the importance which it expected this area to play in its future growth. The company had first become interested in ocean mining in 1961 when it decided to check out some 'pretty wild statements' appearing in the press at the time, claiming that there was a fabulous mineral treasure lying on the ocean floor, just waiting to be picked up. Kennecott's exploration department decided to bring up five or six tons of nodules from a shallow site in 1962 to see if there was any truth to these stories and discovered enough to warrant a further look. The company then had special equipment made for taking samples from the ocean floor and lent this equipment and a technician to any oceanographic institute with a ship going 'anywhere interesting' in the world. In return, the institutes would give Kennecott half of the samples taken and it would do its own analysis. This programme was successful. Kennecott subsequently leased its own boat, gradually charting nodule concentrations in the various oceans of the world. During this period the company also began to do some metallurgical work to devise an efficient process for extracting minerals from the nodules. It began a few feasibility 'looks' (less detailed than feasibility 'studies') on possible methods of mining the nodules.

By the early 1970s Dubs felt that Kennecott had devised an adequate method, in concept, of raising nodules to the surface. Although an artificial seabed had been constructed to study alternative methods of picking up nodules off the ocean floor, a sea trial at full depths had not been carried out. Dubs strongly believed that Kennecott, although ahead of its competitors by as much as several years, badly lacked the 'operational' know-how which could be acquired only by actually using full-size equipment at sea. He thought the company was 'below zero on the learning curve' with its ocean-mining system. The metallurgical process, on the other hand, had been tested in a pilot plant and looked extremely promising. (In fact, Kennecott's 'very elegant' process was one of the reasons why one of the British firms later joined the venture.)

Looking ahead from the vantage point of early 1972, Dubs saw three particular problems that Kennecott faced: he estimated that another $150 million would be needed for development work, plus perhaps $1 billion for a full-scale mining operation including a ship, bottom miner and processing plant. Kennecott could not finance such an undertaking alone. The second problem was actually to develop the technical systems. However, given time and money, he felt that Kennecott could probably accomplish this alone. The third difficulty was to find a way to deal with the political uncertainties which were arising from the Law of the Sea Conference. These three problems led Dubs and Mr Milliken, Kennecott's President, to conclude that they needed to find partners to share the costs of operation. They set a number of parameters for the joint venture:

1. Kennecott would retain 40 per cent ownership of the venture and try to find six partners to take 10 per cent each. This division of ownership would give Kennecott control in all but the most extreme cases, and was all that it could afford, given the magnitude of the proposed expenditures. For a number of important decisions,

such as moving into a new phase of the project (see below), a two-thirds majority would be needed, effectively giving Kennecott veto rights.

2. Since there was no legally recognised mine site, Kennecott decided not to charge its new partners a premium for the work which it had already done, but rather to take a credit for expenses incurred to date. The other companies would pay equal amounts for joint venture expenses until each had contributed an amount equal to Kennecott's total expenditures to date, at which point Kennecott would begin to contribute proportionately as well.

3. Kennecott would be the operator. Dubs would be in charge and Kennecott employees would carry out the project. There would be no separately incorporated joint venture company and thus no joint venture employees. Each partner would be able to write off its share of expenses against its current income. Kennecott would retain all rights to the technology, for uses other than undersea mining.

4. A three-phase work program would be established and, once a company joined, it would be financially committed to complete at least the first phase. The three phases were to be: (i) basic development work, (ii) a full-scale prototype mining ship, and (iii) commercial development. Each firm would be billed quarterly for its share of the costs. Each phase had to be completed on time and within budget to protect the partners. If it were not, unanimous approval would be needed to continue. Commercial development, believed to lie, at best, seven years in the future, would see each firm taking a proportional share of the mine's output.

5. In order to create 'very strong glue' to hold the group of firms together, the venture's assets would be indivisible. If a firm wanted to leave, it would get nothing except what it could sell its shares for to another firm, and any new purchaser would have to be approved by the existing partners. Any firm leaving the group had to stay out of ocean mining for five years.

In December 1972 Dubs began to look for partners for the joint venture. His target was large mining firms which would have the patience and capacity to invest tens of millions of dollars (initially) in a project that would not pay off for many years. Since Kennecott planned to do the work itself, partners without ocean-mining experience were acceptable and, in some ways, preferable. Kennecott also wanted to include non-US partners in the venture; these could lobby their own governments with respect to positions taken in the Law of the Sea Conference, and might possibly convince their governments to enact domestic legislation with respect to seabed development. After presenting its financial proposal, work plans, and an account of developmental work done to date to approximately 20 companies in Japan, France, Germany, Holland, England, Canada and the United States, Kennecott was able to bring together a joint venture group which closely matched its original intentions. The partners were: Kennecott, 50 per cent; Mitsubishi, 10 per cent. Norando, 10 per cent; Consolidated Gold Fields, 10 per cent; and Rio Tinto-Zinc, 20 per cent. Rio Tinto subsequently sold half its shares to British Petroleum. Serious discussants who did not join were US Steel, which wanted more than a 10 per cent share, Union Minière and a group of German firms which Dubs decided were too closely linked with the German government. Each of these firms did ultimately join one or another of the undersea-mining joint ventures.

A committee of representatives with one member from each participant managed the venture. This group met to decide on policies and strategies, and to approve budgets. It gave much of its attention to potential political and legal problems coming out of the Law of the Sea Conference and domestic US legislation, but none at all to detailed technical considerations. Dubs presided over the group as the member representing the 50 per cent partner, and also reported to it, representing Kennecott the operator, which had been hired by the group to carry out the project.

In addition to the committee of representatives, employees from the partners were brought together on 'technical advisory committees'. Any number of these committees could be formed at the request of Kennecott. These committees were created in areas such as ship handling and international taxation, where Kennecott felt it could make use of the expertise of its partners. There was some debate, however, as to the operational usefulness of such committees, and their major role may have been to give the partners a sense of participation in the project.

Ocean Management Inc.

The history of the Ocean Management joint venture began with the work of John Shaw at Inco. As the first general manager of ocean activities within the organisation, Shaw, like Dubs, had a very high profile. He reported directly to the President of Inco, Mr Gagnebin, with a monthly two-page memo.

Shaw headed a tightly-knit group of about twelve engineers and oceanographers located in Bellevue, Washington, far removed from the seat of the organisation. In the early 1970s, this group tested different types of nodule collectors and evaluated different methods of exploring for mine sites. The group felt that it was making very good progress by 1972, although, in the opinion of outsiders, it was clearly lagging behind two other firms, Deepsea Ventures and Kennecott, in its developmental work.

In 1972 Mr Gagnebin retired and John Shaw's new boss, Dr. William Steven, Senior Vice-President, reviewed the future prospects for ocean mining. Like Mr Dubs he concluded that the cost, the diverse technical disciplines involved and the political problems on the horizon made a joint venture attractive. He asked Dean Ramstad, Vice-President, and John Shaw to seek partners and later brought in Jim Finnegan, an engineer and lawyer, to assist in coping with the many legal problems involved in putting together and operating a multi-national consortium devoted to the development of deep-sea mining.

The first candidate Inco considered as a joint venture partner was Deepsea Ventures Inc., at the time a subsidiary of Tenneco. Deepsea, under the direction of Jack Flipse, had been the ocean-mining pioneer and was definitely the early leader in the field. In 1973, Flipse was looking for a group of partners to put up $20 million (thus matching what Deepsea had already spent), to fund an at-sea mining test. However, after six months or so of bargaining (during which, Flipse claimed, he was giving the Inco executives a free education in undersea mining), it became clear that Deepsea was really looking for backers, not partners, and wanted someone who would put up the money and stay out of the way. This was not the role Inco intended for itself. (Deepsea was eventually purchased by US Steel and thus became part of the Ocean Mining Associate joint venture.)

Inco next considered the three German companies (which had formed a joint venture known as AMR) that Dubs had talked to when setting up the Kennecott group. Inco felt that the German companies might make suitable partners because they had some technical expertise, particularly in mine site selection, yet they would be unlikely to want to dominate the venture since both the mine site and processing plant would be so far from Germany. Metallgesellschaft, the founding member of AMR, was a very large German mining company which had become interested in undersea mining in the mid-1960s and had participated in several exploration cruises with Deepsea Ventures. In its enthusiasm for undersea mining, Metallgesellschaft had then interested the German government in supporting a major research programme, which it agreed to fund provided other German firms were involved as well. Preussag, a company with oil as well as mineral interests and considerable offshore experience, then joined Metallgesell-schaft to do more work with Deepsea and some laboratory-scale processing work in Frankfurt. Shortly afterwards, however, the two German firms parted company with Deepsea, feeling that much more work needed to be done on mine site location, while the Americans believed top priority should be given to the development of a mining system. The Germans were also uncomfortable with the new and untried metallurgical separation process which the Americans wanted to use. Finally, it had become clear to the Germans that Deepsea was really looking for a financial backer, not a participating partner, a sentiment to be echoed by Inco two years later.

In 1971, with the addition of Saltzgitter, a diversified German steel company, and with heavy support from the German government, the German group outfitted the ship *Valdivia*, creating the most advanced ocean-mining research vessel in the world. The following year, the Valdivia embarked on a major voyage to the Pacific to carry out a detailed study on nodule concentrations and competition. This trip confirmed that the major nodule reserves were in the Pacific – unfortunate from the Germans' point of view, in that this was far from their home base. By early 1973, the Germans recognised that massive amounts of capital would be needed to mine the seas and that there would be considerable technical difficulties in developing a success-ful mining system. The group decided it was time to find a North American partner.

Inco and the German companies agreed in principle in 1974 to establish a joint venture. Sumitomo, one of the largest industrial complexes in Japan, which like Inco had previously considered a joint arrangement with Deepsea, was now invited by Inco to join the negotia-tions to form OMI. Apart from having considerable terrestrial mining experience, Sumitomo had been involved in the development by Dr J. Mero of a continuous line bucket system. Sumitomo formed a group of twenty-three Japnese companies, which incorporated a management company named Domco, soon after establishment of the OMI joint venture. The participants agreed to continue the search for a US partner to round out the venture. The parameters of the joint venture were as follows:

1. Each firm would have an equal ownership percentage and all decisions would be unanimous. Thus, each firm would hold veto

power. All costs would be shared equally.

2. A five-year programme was planned to carry out a feasibility study detailing the cost of a complete mining system and the mineral prices which would be necessary to make it economical. Finding a decent mine site, developing and testing a mining system and a recovery process were all part of the project.

Most of 1974 was spent deciding which firms would undertake various parts of the project and how much funding would be allocated to each. A two-tiered responsibility system was established in which one participating firm or the joint-venture general manager would be given primary ('R') responsibility for a task, while others with relevant skills or a particular interest would be given an associate ('A') position. The firm with R responsibility could carry out the work itself or subcontract it. Table 3.2 presents some examples of the way in which tasks were divided among the participants.

3. There were to be no charges for work done by any of the firms prior to the formation of the venture. Any firm with existing patents relevant to the project (there were 21 of these) would grant a royalty-free, non-exclusive licence to the venture to use such patents. Patents developed by participants while acting for the joint venture would be granted to the venture on an exclusive, royalty-free basis, although the firm registering the patent could control its use in other than ocean-mining applications. Twelve of these patents were obtained.

Ocean Management Inc. established itself in Inco's Bellevue offices under the direction of John Shaw. He also continued to manage Inco's own ocean-mining department, located in the same building. Shaw reported to a joint venture committee of four executives, one from each participating company, which met every 2–3 months. Five other employees (later six) were seconded from the participants and brought in sub-projects, some of which are identified in Figure 3.1. Each sub-project was the responsibility of a manager from the R-designated company who worked together with managers from the A firm for the particular project. Interfaces between the sub-project groups were managed by the seconded employees at Bellevue. Figure 3.1 presents an organisation chart for the joint venture. Other major task categories included Marketing Analysis, Law of the Sea, Programme Control and Budget Administration, and Conceptual Design.

In November 1975 Sedco Inc., a Dallas company with approximately $200 million in sales which specialised in the construction and

Table 3.2: Ocean Management Inc. Sample Task Responsibilities

Exploration	Individual Company[a] A B C D				Joint Venture Manager
1. Provide and operate exploration vessels	R				
2. Recommend pilot test sites	A	A	A	A	R
3. Verify plot sites	R	A	A	A	
4. Obtain 5 tons of nodules etc.	R	A			
Mining					
1. Evaluation of possible systems, report every six months	A	A	A	A	R
2. Design and construct pipeline	A	R			
3. Design and construct pumps	R	A	A	A	
4. Design and construct air lift system	R				
5. Design, construct, and test collectors	A	R	A	A	
6. Pilot mining ship					
(a) Preliminary design	A	A	A	R	
(b) Acquire and modify ship	A	A	A	R	
(c) Operate pilot ship	A	A	A	R	
Processing					
1. Bench-scale testing	A	R	A	A	
2. Recommend a final process: remaining process responsibility will be determined after process is chosen	A	R	A	A	

Note: a. After the fourth company, Sedco, had joined OMI.

Figure 3.1: Ocean Management, Inc. Organization Chart [a]

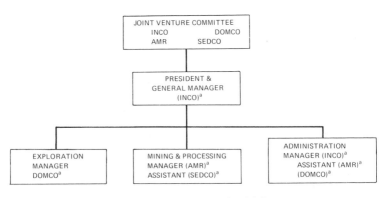

Note: a. Original employer of individual. See Table 3.2 for corporate responsibilities.

operation of semi submersible oil-drilling rigs, joined Ocean Manage--
ment Inc. Because of its expertise, the company was given R responsibility for the design and construction of a pilot mining ship (a conver-
sion of one of the company's existing ships), for the specification and
procurement of pipe-handling equipment and for the development of
systems to transfer nodules from a mining ship to an ore carrier. Gil
Clements, the President of Sedco, joined the joint venture committee.

Analysis – Inco Versus Kennecott

These two companies, faced with similar tasks, chose to establish very
different joint ventures. Kennecott's objective was to bring in partners
who would provide financial and political support, yet at the same
time to keep for itself control of the overall direction and pace of the
venture, and its day to day technical work. It clearly wanted to establish a dominant parent joint venture with itself as the dominant parent.
Inco on the other hand wanted technical as well as financial and political support from its partners and chose to establish a shared management venture. The most obvious differences in design between the two
ventures were as follows:

1. *Ownership Percentages.* The Inco participants had equal holdings,
   while Kennecott and its partners had very unequal holdings.
2. *Veto Powers.* In the Inco venture, each partner had the right of
   veto; in the Kennecott venture, only Kennecott did.
3. *Work Allocation.* In the Inco venture, work was shared among all
   partners – albeit not equally – whereas Kennecott was the sole
   operator in its venture.
4. *Previous work.* In the Inco venture, no charge was made for work
   done by any participant prior to the formation of the venture,
   even though some firms had clearly done more than others.
   This established the principle of equal partnership. In the Kennecott venture, only Kennecott received credit for work done prior
   to the establishment of the venture, a reflection of the company's
   advanced technical expertise.

It seems clear that Kennecott's desire for a dominant parent joint
venture stemmed from its position of technical leadership at the time.
Dubs believed that there were few, if any, partners that Kennecott
could have included in its venture which had ocean mining skills that

Kennecott did not already match. However, in choosing mining companies as partners (necessary so that each could take a share of the mineral output), Dubs acquired partners who did have related skills. Not all of these partners were prepared to play as passive a role as Kennecott had intended for them. One British executive said: 'We did not intend to simply become a banker for Kennecott.' These companies expected to make their technical input into the venture through the technical advisory committee. However, in the words of a manager from a second British firm, 'just as this committee was starting to get some real teeth Kennecott disbanded it and replaced it with workshops which were convened only at Kennecott's discretion'. According to this executive, Kennecott's engineers were generally somewhat defensive when making presentations to their partners: 'Let's put it this way: for Kennecott a good meeting was one in which they were not caught out; they had all their sums done properly – whereas in our view a good meeting might have been one in which the Americans learned something.'

With time, Kennecott's domination of the venture eased somewhat. British Petroleum s ship-handling expertise was acknowledged and utilised. After two years of debate the partners' views on the way to raise nodules to the ocean surface were given some credence. In 1979, for the first time, a significant piece of work was subcontracted to one of the partners, when Consolidated Gold Fields was given the task of carrying out a study to predict the cost of land-based nickel production in the 1980s and 1990s. By 1980 the activities of the group had slowed to a crawl, in part because no US legislation had been passed and the Law of the Sea Conference looked very discouraging, but also because of changes within Kennecott itself, described below.

This case study suggests that there may be two types of dangers in using a dominant parent joint venture in such a complex and long-term situation. The first danger is obvious: the dominant parent is betting that its managerial and technical skills will be adequate, without help from its partners, for the task at hand. If it is wrong, the venture will have difficulties and may fail. Judging the adequacy of one's skills is a straightforward managerial task and Kennecott considered this in setting up the venture. In retrospect, Kennecott may have been slightly over optimistic in assessing its skills, although it is impossible to be certain. Once a firm decides to play a dominant-parent role, it must find a partner (or group of partners) to play a passive role. Kennecott did not quite manage to find such a group, but probably to its benefit.

The second danger in using a dominant parent joint venture is more subtle and relates to the long-term commitment necessary to see such a project through to its completion. If only one firm provides the driving force, as is the case in dominant parent joint ventures, any change in management or attitude within the firm can quickly slow or halt the venture. There will be no strongly committed and knowledgeable partners who could provide continuing motivation. Such a change in attitude took place within Kennecott as the result of a change in senior management. The new management instituted a cost-cutting drive just as Kennecott's partners had finally 'caught up' with Kennecot in their payments into the venture and it was time for Kennecott to start paying its proportional share again. Dubs no longer had the luxury of playing the role of both operator and owner on behalf of Kennecott. He now had to report to the Kennecott corporate office just as he did to the other partners. As a part of its cost-cutting programme, Kennecott decided not to start making the payments it owed, but rather to let its ownership position slide from 50 to 40 per cent (the original goal), while that of each of the other partners increased from 10 to 12 per cent. Coincident with these changes within Kennecott, the activities within the venture slowed dramatically. Given the political situation, this may have been appropriate. Nevertheless this set of circumstances shows the danger of using a dominant parent joint venture in a long-term speculative situation in which there will inevitably be good times and bad times.

At first sight, Inco's venture looks like a prescription for managerial disaster. The combination of four disparate partners, each with equal voting rights and the power of veto seems a sure formula for failure. That it was not a disaster was due largely to the extensive negotiations which took place before the venture was formed, as well as the partners' determination that the project succeed. The overall technical task was divided into a series of individual projects, only one or two of which (notably the collector system) were truly joint developments. Thus while the management and co-ordination of the venture were shared, the majority of the work was carried out by single companies, on a predetermined project basis.

However, the joint venture committee was a truly joint body, and somewhat unwieldy, as it was difficult even to find a meeting time suitable for four senior executives in different companies and countries. In addition, each participating company had a very different internal decision-making process. While Gil Clements could speak for Sedco and make decisions on the spot in committee meetings, other executives had to report to head offices and in some cases go through a rather cumbersome process before reporting back to the committee. Since some firms were under tighter budget constraints than others, there were differences of opinion as to how fast to proceed and resistance by some partners to spending more money as the cost of the programme rose significantly above the original estimates. A few parts of the project were cancelled.

One advantage to having the cumbersome joint venture committee was the greater impetus to work out problems at a lower level. Faced with disagreement between technical personnel of two participants, a manager at OMI could speed up resolution by telling the disputants that if they could not agree, he would have to take the matter to the joint venture committee. Although one individual described the OMI employees as a 'bunch of company representatives sent to spy on one another and to make sure that no company was profiting at the expense of the others', most were quite happy with the arrangement, stating that each company wanted to be seen in the best possible light and therefore sent very good employees to work for OMI and the project teams. One OMI manager commented:

> We made a few decisions based on politics rather than economics — because of the company they came from rather than because they were most qualified, but such decisions were very few, especially given the nature of the joint venture.
>
> I remember one instance when we were at sea and the nodule collector we were testing broke. Should we repair it, or try a different design which we also had on board? Emotions surrounding a decision like that can run rather high when each design was done by a group from a different company. Those stresses would not be present to the same extent in a one-company operation.
>
> I should not overemphasize these problems. They were minor in comparison with the benefits we got from having partners. In a project like this, you need to have someone challenging your thinking and helping you from a technical point of view. If you set up a venture in which your partners' only interests are financial, then all they will do is criticize you (the operator) on financial grounds. This is unlikely to improve the venture — and cost over-runs are inevitable.

Conclusion

It is not clear that either of these joint ventures outperformed the other, although Kennecott's technical lead did disappear over the period. As of 1980, both ventures have severely reduced their operations and are losing potentially valuable personnel as they cut back. It remains to be seen which venture will be able to respond most effectively when external conditions improve. One observation that can be made is that the ventures were not the pure archetypes of dominant parent and of shared management ventures they would appear to be to the outsider. The Kennecott venture, particularly by 1980, was not so dominated by Kennecott as one might expect from looking at the ownership figures. Due to the creation of separate project responsibilities, Inco's venture was never so 'shared' a venture as it could have been, and this made it easier to manage. There is clearly a large and fruitful middle ground between the extremes of the dominant parent and the totally-shared management ventures.

The ocean mining story is far from over. The resource is so large that it seems certain to be tapped eventually. Countries may have a longer time horizon than companies, but even they will ultimately see the need for action. However, before the oceans are mined, there may be a significant realignment of joint venture partners. One British executive stated that he thought it very likely that the final Law of the Sea Treaty would make ocean mining unattractive for private companies, but that some countries, notably Japan and possibly Germany, would attach such importance to the minerals that they would subsidise their companies to mine them. Joint ventures would be recreated on a national basis. If this scenario comes to pass, and it is significant that Japan has already succeeded in forming a domestic venture, 1980 may prove to be the end of the first phase of joint venture activity in ocean mining.

The major product of this phase has been knowledge, and the companies with the smallest shares in the joint venture have acquired it most cheaply. Part of this knowledge relates to the mining of manganese nodules and, secrecy agreements notwithstanding, each partner will carry this knowledge to any new venture it might join. As one executive explained, 'it's very difficult to sue someone for knowing enough *not* to try certain techniques for recovering manganese nodules.' From their experience to date, some of the participants have learned a great deal about the formation and management of joint ventures, and it will be interesting to see how this knowledge is reflected in any new relationships which are formed. The general manager of one ocean-mining venture commented on his own learning experience:

> I am certainly less naïve now than I was when we started this venture. The major issues are not technical. They are interpersonal. The important thing about a joint venture is that it forms the context in which people from different firms are to work together. It's easy to get it wrong. The trick is to adjust with circumstances.

Postscript

On April 30, 1982, the Law of the Sea Conference adopted a final treaty, but it was such that it seemed more likely to halt undersea mining than encourage it. The treaty specified that there would be production limits imposed on mining companies and that five would have to pass on their mining and possibly ship-positioning technology to Third World countries. As a result, most consortia have only a few active personnel and very limited spending plans. The following estimates were published by David Tonge of the Financial Times of London:

Table 3.3: Spending Estimates

Group	Spending to Date ($ Millions)	1982 Budget ($ Millions)
1. Ocean Mining Associates (U.S. Steel Group)	100	10
2. Ocean Management Inc. (Inco Group)	60	2
3. Ocean Minerals Co. (Lockheed Group)	120	5
4. Kennecott Group	50	1
5. Afernod	40	16

Source: David Tonge, *Financial Times.*

4 HOW TO DESIGN A SHARED MANAGEMENT JOINT VENTURE

It must be clear by now that I do not believe a firm should enter a shared management venture unless it is absolutely necessary. This chapter contains guidelines for deciding when a shared management venture really is necessary, and it presents suggestions for designing such a venture so as to maximise its chances of success. The elements of joint venture design considered in this chapter are the choice of a partner, staffing, and designing a reward system for the parents. The title of the chapter is a slight misnomer, as dominant parent ventures are discussed herein, particularly in the section on staffing, and the comments on product flows between parents and ventures apply to both types of venture.

When to Use One

If nothing else, I hope that this book, and in particular this chapter, will prevent firms from entering shared management ventures by accident. Quite a number of companies seem to drift into shared management ventures by default, not realising what they are doing, or that there is any important difference between a venture in which one parent dominates and that in which each plays an equal role. A shared management venture should not be established unless it is abundantly clear that the extra benefit of having two parents managerially involved will more than offset the extra difficulty which will result. This is a critical question which it seems all too few firms bother to ask. As one manager quoted later in the chapter put it, you've got to have a 'very large carrot' to keep both parents committed during the tough periods.

In order to decide if a shared management venture is necessary, an analysis of what each partner is bringing to the venture is required. If one partner is contributing only what I have labelled either attributes or assets, then that partner should play a passive role in the venture and allow the other to dominate. Its managerial contribution is not important. Typical assets and attributes are listed below.

Assets	Attributes
1. Capital	1. Nationality
2. Trademarks	2. Source of raw material or
3. Patents	component supply
	3. Customer for venture output

The essential point to be made about these assets and attributes is that *while they may be necessary to the joint venture's success, they do not require managerial involvement on the part of the parent supplying them.* So the critical question for joint venture design is not who is supplying which assets, but rather which partner has the managerial skills and knowledge that the venture is going to require to be successful. As shown in Table 4.1, if either parent has no relevant managerial skills or knowledge (for instance, no knowledge of the country, market or technology in question) then the situation is relatively clear-cut. No joint venture should be formed unless the other parent has all of the required skills and knowledge and, if formed, the venture should be dominated by that parent. In such a situation it should be relatively easy to convince the partner without the managerial skills to play the passive role. Further discussion on the role of a passive parent is contained in Chapter Eight.

If both parents are bringing relevant knowledge or skill to the venture the situation is more complex. If each brings complementary and partial knowledge — for instance if one firm has a knowledge of technology, the other a knowledge of the market — then a shared management venture is the necessary solution. This is particularly true if the technology is changing or needs adaptation for the venture's market. If the technology is static and simple to apply to the new market, the venture may be able to operate successfully without ongoing managerial input from the technology supplying parent.

The most complex situations arise when one parent has all of the necessary managerial skills and knowledge and the other has at least some, and possibly all as well. The tendency is to form a shared management venture (based not on complementary skills but overlapping ones), when strictly speaking a dominant parent venture is all that is required. Since it may prove impossible to convince either parent to play a totally passive role, I would recommend that the venture be 'shared', but to try and control the areas in which sharing takes place. Specifically, I would recommend that the venture's board of directors (a 'shared' body) be given responsibility for the strategic direction of the venture, but that one parent dominate the venture's operating side.

Table 4.1: Selecting a Joint Venture Type

	Firm A Relevant Managerial Skills and Knowledge		
	None	Partial	Complete
None	No joint venture	No joint venture	Venture dominated by Firm A
Partial	No joint venture	Shared management venture	Share strategic management if necessary. Firm A dominates operations
	Firm B Relevant Managerial Skills and Knowledge		
Complete	Venture dominated by Firm B	Share strategic management if necessary. Firm B dominates operations	Share strategic management only. Either parent dominates operations

In other words, only one parent would supply functional managers, and the board would not get involved in day to day activities, giving the general manager as much autonomy as possible. These issues are further discussed in Chapter Eight, and the importance of autonomy is demonstrated in Chapter Five.

Using a guide like Table 4.1 is complicated by the fact that the importance of a partner's managerial contribution will probably change over time. As was illustrated in Chapter Two, what seems like a critical skill today can be less important two years hence. All of this is by way of saying that this scheme is no replacement for good managerial judgement. It does, however, identify the key issues on which a manager should be focusing.

One direct implication of Table 4.1 is that dominant parent joint ventures should be used when a firm is taking a partner *only* because it is being forced to by the local government. If the foreign partner does not need either the managerial skills or any of the attributes of the local partner, except its nationality, it should find ways to manage the joint venture without interference, regardless of the relative owner-ship positions. In such a situation foreign firms often prefer to find a local passive firm which has no knowledge of the product in question. They reason that if there is no possibility that the local partner will learn the joint venture's business their bargaining position with the local government will remain strong. One president whose company had set up more than ten ventures in developing countries made this point very forcefully. He would (now) only choose as partners companies which: (i) knew nothing about his firm's line of business; (ii) were neither government agencies nor directly controlled by the government; (iii) would be willing to play the role of a passive investor.

Unfortunately, specifying the selection criteria for a partner in a shared management joint venture is not as straightforward.

Choosing a Partner

Making recommendations about choosing a partner is a little like advising your daughter on the kind of man she should marry. Everyone's taste is different, and the ideal partner for one marriage may be a disaster in another. One of the greatest problems with partner selection is that many of the characteristics which one might be willing to agree are generally desirable, such as honesty, dependability and trustworthiness, typically only become evident in times of stress, such as in the middle of a crisis three years after the venture has been formed. For these reasons trying to create a shopping list of desirable partner characteristics does not appear to be a useful exercise. As a result, this research did not focus on questions of partner selection, although conversations with managers and a review of the literature did suggest a number of ideas that seem worthy of review. These are put forward as hypotheses, propositions which seem sensible but which have not been empirically tested. They are as follows:

1. The more similar the culture of firms forming a shared management joint venture, the easier the venture will be to manage. Culture is considered to have two components, one being the culture of the country in which a company is based, the other the 'corporate culture' of the particular firm in question.
2. The more similar in size are the parents of a shared management venture, the easier the venture will be to manage. A significant size mismatch between a venture's parents can create a lot of problems for the venture.

The Effects of Cultural Differences

It is probably safe to say that if a joint venture is to be successful its managers will have to develop into an effective, cohesive, operational team. And to be effective, managers need to be able to evaluate one another's judgements. The production manager has to learn how to treat an estimate from the sales manager, while the sales manager has to be able to evaluate the engineer's estimates of the time required to complete a product modification, and so on. This collective skill, which has been labelled a company's 'core skill'[1] is likely to be more difficult to develop if the managers in the venture come from both parents rather than just one. If may be particularly difficult if the parent firms are of different nationality and of markedly different corporate culture. The greater the cultural gap between the firms forming the venture, the more difficult it will be to create the required cohesion.

Managers of different nationality may have differing attitudes to such basic things as the desirability of material wealth, the importance of on-the-job performance, or the desirability of change. The greater the cultural gap between the parents' base countries, the greater the problem. A fundamental hindrance to the creation of a core skill can simply be the difference in language. Many joint ventures formed in Japan in the 1960s between Japanese and North American firms failed in the early 1970s. Cultural differences were cited as a major problem in many of these. One could predict similar problems in shared management ventures formed between firms from the developed and developing worlds.

Managers are conditioned not only by the culture of the country in which they were raised, but also by the company for which they have been working prior to their placement in the joint venture. It seems, for instance, quite possible that a manager in a British oil company might have more in common with a counterpart in an American oil company than in, say, a small British retail firm. Unfortunately, researchers have not yet devised a means of measuring differences in corporate culture, or personality, although managers are often well aware of such differences and can describe them in considerable detail. The president of one Canadian venture, which contained functional executives from three companies, made the following comment.

The differences in corporate background show up in a number of ways. In one division I discovered I had really insulted a senior manager by going directly to a subordinate to get some specific information. In his previous company, the hierarchy was very strictly observed and if you wanted information you asked at the top and the request was relayed down until someone could answer. Then the answer came all the way back up. I'm used to an operation where you can go directly to the man who can answer the question. Employees of another division are disgruntled with the bureaucracy they find here. They are used to a small entrepreneurial organiza-tion. What we regard as the facts of life, like the time taken to get an approval, they look at with surprise and dismay.

This comment suggests that size can have an effect on corporate culture, an idea which is discussed subsequently. Many managers also see a relationship between a firm's industry and its culture. Steel com-panies have different personalities than retailers, and both of these are very different from land-developers or oil companies, to name but a few. One cannot push this idea too far, however, as all companies in an industry do not see themselves as having the same personality.

Although I would argue that joint ventures between firms in the same industry will be easier to manage than those between parents from different industries, there is an important caveat to be observed. As indicated earlier in this chapter, joint ventures between firms with similar skills and knowledge can tend to cause difficulties. Two joint ventures in this study suffered from acrimonious board debates because each of the parents felt that it was the expert at producing the product in question or selling in the chosen country. Since neither would acknowledge the other's expertise, a great amount of time was spent in dispute, with no beneficial result.

Of the twelve failed ventures in this study, two were ascribed to 'differences in corporate personality', none to differences in national culture.

The Effects of Differences in Parental Size

Size mismatches between parents can contribute to differences in corporate culture which may affect a venture's performance. However, such mismatches can also have a much more direct effect on a venture. The most widely publicised of these relates to the provision of capital to the venture. If a joint venture is to grow quickly, it typically requires infusions of cash. Very often the small parent will be unable to put up such cash while the larger parent may be eager to. Even as I write this, the Canadian subsidiary of a large US multinational firm is taking its much smaller Canadian partner to court in an attempt to dissolve their joint venture, apparently because the local partner is only interested in short-term profits and will not make the long-term invest-ment in the venture that the business requires. An earlier attempt by the subsidiary to buy out the Canadian firm's interest in the venture was not successful.

Another problem which can arise when a joint venture is small in size compared to one of its parents is that it may have difficulty attracting that parent's attention. A venture may be critically important to its small parent and insignificant to the larger one. Thus, executives of the larger parent may not be available so quickly or so often as those of the small parent and may not have time to give much thought to the joint venture's problems. The following quotes are from managers of small companies involved in joint ventures with much larger partners, taken from a 1976 study by Adler and Hlavacek:[2]

> The small company worked eight days a week to get the joint venture formed while the larger parent dragged its feet and needed many levels of review or decision.
>
> The large company, especially its technical people, saw the joint venture as an admission of inability or failure on its own part. Small companies' technical people are generally more receptive. They know they can't do everything themselves and therefore keep their eyes and ears wide open for any new development on the outside that they could possibly use.

Of course the executives of the larger firms had their own perspective on the situation: 'The executives at the much smaller parent are difficult to do business with. They have no interest in or time for our detailed planning studies, except in the area of profitability.'

Staffing the Venture

Staffing is one of the few areas in this research project in which I had a clear set of expectations about what I would find, before I began talking to managers. I expected that the designers of shared management ventures would face a staffing dilemma. They would be forced to make a choice between using functional managers from one parent or bringing them in from both parents. As I saw it, each option would have some severe disadvantages, as well as very distinct advantages. Staffing from both parents would hinder the development of a core skill but facilitate good communications and information transfer from both parents to the venture. This would be important to a venture in which both parents had valuable knowledge and skill to offer. If, on the other hand, staffing was done with executives from a single parent, core skill development would be facilitated, but communication with the other parent would be severely hampered. This would be a good solution in a dominant parent venture but would cause problems in a shared management venture.

As it turned out, few managers seemed to feel that this was as critical or as delicate a choice as I did. Overwhelmingly they opted, in shared management ventures, to use managers from both parents when they could. The statistics below show that 11 of 19 shared management ventures used functional executives from both parents. This is hardly an overwhelming statistic, but most of the eight shared management ventures listed in Table 4.2 as not using employees from both parents were either too small to have any full-time employees (and thus used employees from the local parent on a part-time basis, together with visits from foreign parent personnel) or had previously used employees from both parents but over time had learned enough to be able to dispense with the expensive foreigners. One American company had a very difficult time finding employees to send to its Swedish venture (the problems were both language and the Swedish tax rate) and was relieved when enough Swedes became trained in the technology for it to be no longer necessary. There was no significant difference in performance between ventures which did use employees from both parents (a success rate of 55 per cent) and those which did not (a success rate of 50 per cent).

Discussions with managers in these ventures indicated that I had overestimated the cultural differences to be found between managers in ventures whose parents were for the most part Canadian, American and North-Western European (Swedish, German, French and British) firms. To find the type of differences that I was expecting, one would probably have to examine ventures encompassing wider cultural extremes. This notion was reinforced by the fact that the ventures in which the problems of mixed staffing did make themselves felt were Iranian–American and Italian–American. The venture in Iran was performing very poorly until a new general manager sent most of the Americans in the venture back home. They had not been able to adapt to dealing with a workforce which had, on average, the education of an American 8-year old. These managers were replaced with Iranians who were first sent for short training periods (three weeks to two months) with the US parent. Performance improved considerably. The other problem situation involved an American who saw himself as an organised, worker-oriented manager trying to maximise medium- and long-term profits, forced to work with a group of Italian managers whom he considered to be disorganised, overly concerned with the short term, paying too much attention to market share and too little to

Table 4.2: Staffing

	Source of General Manager			Source of Functional Managers			
	Local Parent	Foreign Parent	Other	One Parent	One Parent and/or Outsiders	Both Parents	Neither Parent
Dominant Parent	12	1	–	6	5	2	–
Shared Management	11	4	4	2	6	11	–
Independent	2	–	2	–	2	–	2

profitability. They would 'do anything' to get a sale. As a result of these differences, the American told the Italians less and less about what he was doing and tried to manage his part of the venture as if the rest did not exist. After several years of poor performance, he was replaced.

In sharp contrast to these two ventures were several whose managers complained because their ventures did not have mixed staffing. One Canadian manager specifically blamed the demise of his venture on the fact that the technology supplying UK parent had not sent a full-time technical man to the Canadian venture. Trying to explain to the British by telex, telephone and letter that the British technology needed to be modified somewhat for the venture to be successful caused such a delay that competition was able to enter the market first, ultimately preventing the venture from obtaining the market share it needed for survival. Poor information transfer was the exception rather than the rule in this study, as over 80 per cent of the managers who said that information transfer was important also stated that it was well done.

The other manager who complained because his venture did not have mixed staffing was the American mentioned in Chapter Two who wanted to gain more influence over his UK venture which was being dominated by his British partner. The Americans had marketing skills which they believed would help the venture but, without one of their managers in the joint company, they simply could not make themselves heard.

A final example of interest involves the odd practice of using mixed staffing in a dominant venture. In one Canadian venture the foreign parent, which was the dominant parent, wanted a local manager in charge, apparently to curry favour with the local government. Partly as a result of this staffing decision, the venture became one of only two dominant parent ventures in this study which failed. The general manager explained the impotence which he felt in this position.

> I was in a very peculiar and often frustrating position, since I did not control the major parameters of the business. We made most of our purchases (from the dominant parent) at a price fixed by them, and we sold nearly all our output to them, again at their price. Product mix, and even the production schedule, were beyond my control. My number two man reported to his superiors in Germany (disguised location) every day; but because of the language problem, I never knew exactly what was being discussed. Because of the difference in parent pay scales, he was even being paid more than I was.

Staffing is clearly an important part of the design of a joint venture. My conclusions with respect to joint venture staffing are:

1. Dominant parent joint ventures should not employ managers from their passive parents.
2. To enhance information flow and capture the skills of parent companies, shared management ventures between firms from similar cultures should employ managers from both parents. Core skill development is unlikely to be severely hindered.
3. More research is needed before a conclusion can be drawn with respect to the staffing of shared management ventures between parents of significantly different cultures.

Designing the Reward System

Pay-offs to joint venture partners can take many forms, and are of course an important part of joint venture design. The usual forms of pay-off are dividends, management fees, technical fees or royalties, profits on goods sold to the venture, and possibly a below-market price on goods purchased from the venture. The control aspects of these devices were discussed in Chapter Two and for convenience the pay-off summary presented in that chapter has been reproduced here.

The patterns revealed here are not surprising. In dominant parent ventures all management fees and most of the technical fees paid by the venture go to the dominant parent. However, the passive parent is more likely to be a buyer or seller of goods to the venture, and this function is in many cases the reason the passive parent was invited into the

Table 4.3: Joint Venture Pay-offs

	Percentage of Parent Firms Receiving Each Type of Pay-off					
	Manage-ment Fee	Technical Fee	Dividend	Goods Sold to Venture	Goods Purchased From Venture	Tech. Used as Initial Equity
Dominant Parent Ventures						
Dominant Parents	25%	25%	31%	15%	15%	33%
Passive Parents	0%	15%	31%	31%	23%	33%
Share Management Ventures						
Local Parents	28%	11%	35%	20%	30%	33%
Foreign Parents	16%	58%	35%	55%	15%	37%

venture. In shared management ventures, it is typically the foreign parent which receives a technical fee, and the local partner is more likely than the foreign to receive a management fee. In every case but one, the management fee paid to the local partner was offset by a technical fee paid to the foreign partner. It seemed likely that such fees were in part a method of distributing venture profits in a pre-tax, rather than post-tax, form (i.e. dividends), and not necessarily a payment for specific functions performed. However, such balanced payments did not always work out the way the participants intended. In one case, the foreign parent received a technical fee which was a percentage of sales, while the local firm received a management fee which was a percentage of profits. Because the product was manufactured from a petroleum derivative, its price skyrocketed in the 1970s, while profit as a percentage of sales (although not in absolute terms) fell. As a result, the foreign parent was receiving an income stream approximately five times that of the local parent. This was definitely not the original intent of the partners. Although this particular situation had not been renegotiated, approximately 15 per cent of the ventures reported that the pay-offs to their parents had been significantly renegotiated, and one-third reported minor renegotiations.

Firms with technology to contribute to a joint venture may be able to give it as equity, receive an ongoing technical fee for it, or try for both. Full information was available on 19 such situations and in seven the technology supplying parent both contributed technology as equity and received a technical fee. Five companies claimed only a technical and seven contributed technology only in exchange for equity. One foreign parent, although receiving both equity for its technology and a technical fee, was doing technical work for the venture which cost far more than it was receiving in fees. A senior manager explained the situation, which he estimated was costing his company approximately $300,000 per year.

> Typically, the joint venture will telex to ask us if a new product formulation is possible, and for a quote which they can pass on to their customer. There is not time for us to say 'it will cost us so much to answer this question and prepare the quote – are you willing to pay for it?'; if we took the time, they would lose the customer. As a result, we do the work for nothing as often as not. We also spend a lot of time training their people and doing R&D work for them.
>
> The situation is very different for the local parent. The joint venture might ask them to write some computer programs. Before doing so, the parent prepares a cost estimate, which the venture has to approve, and the venture will be charged if the work is done. The American parent does nothing free.

This company was unusual in the amount of unreimbursed work it performed, but it was not alone in doing such work. Six companies stated that they did a 'significant' amount of work for which they were not paid by their joint venture; eleven acknowledged a 'minor' amount, and five stated they did none at all.

Dividends are also an important method of removing funds from a joint venture. The advantage of dividends is that they focus each parent's attention on the bottom line, and they are not generally paid until the venture is successful. Thus, if the parent's only return is via dividends, the joint venture is not likely to be neglected. However, dividends may not be tax deductible, as fees are, and thus can be a very expensive form of payment. The other problem, if dividends are used as the sole form of pay-off, is that they will create an inappropriate division of pay-offs to the partners, except in that rare circumstance in which the ownership split accurately reflects the contribution made by each parent to the success of the venture. Approximately one-third of the ventures paid dividends, and virtually all of those which did so were more than five years old.

Approximately 40 per cent of the ventures in this study reported that they were involved in significant product transactions with either or both of their parents. Buying from or selling to a joint venture is often perceived to be a good method of getting economic benefit from

Table 4.4: Performance and Product Flows[a]

Product Flows with Parent	Dominant Parent		Shared Management	
	Successful[b]	Liquidated or Reorganised	Successful	Liquidated or Reorganised
Major	3	1	3	5
Minor	4	0	6	2
None	3	0	1	2
Total	10	1	10	9

Notes: a. Data were not available for all 37 ventures, and independent ventures were included with shared management ventures. b. This means only that the venture was neither liquidated nor reorganised due to poor performance.

a venture, but it is a complex procedure which can have a number of unintended side effects. One conclusion of this study is that *the fewer product flows there are between a venture and its parents, the letter off the venture will be.* A 'clean' venture (no product flows with either parent) offers less opportunity for real or perceived unfairness in pay-offs between parents and fosters easier working relationships for all concerned. The evidence which led to this conclusion is presented in this chapter, beginning with the statistics shown in Table 4.4, which indicate that 50 per cent of the ventures which had significant product flows with their parent(s) were liquidated or reorganised due to poor performance, whereas this was only true for 22 per cent of ventures with minor or no product transactions with their parents. Five of eight shared management ventures with major product flows failed, and furthermore, two of the three successful shared management ventures which had significant product flows with their parents were reported by their managers to be performing poorly.

Clearly, avoiding product flows with parent firms is not enough to guarantee the success of a shared management venture, but it does appear to improve the odds.

There are three situations which seem to result in significant product flows between a joint venture and its parents. These are: (i) when a joint venture is formed by a multinational firm which has rationalised its production and tranships components from one plant to another; (ii) when the venture is formed to achieve economies of scale in the creation of a product used by its parents, and thus sells all or most of its output to its parents; and (iii) when the venture is formed to assemble knocked down goods supplied by its foreign parent, to be sold to its local parent, which is the local distributor for the product. Each of these situations is discussed in some detail in this chapter, to explore the complexities inherent in these situations and thus shed some light on the high failure rate.

Problems With Product Flows

The Rationalised Multinational Firm

Multinational firms which have rationalised their production operations, creating a network of specialised plants which tranship components or intermediate products from one to the other, are not good candidates for joint ventures. These firms typically determine transfer prices, product mix, production rates and inventory levels on the basis of optimising earnings for the whole system, rather than for any particular operation. A local firm which becomes a joint venture partner with a multinational to share ownership of one production plant in such a system is unlikely to be able to exert much influence over any of these variables, and thus the profitability of the joint venture will be completely beyond its control. Even if the majority ownership of the venture were held by the local partner it would be of little use as a bargaining weapon, since all important materials coming into the plant will come from the multinational, and all important markets will be other units of the multinational firm, which would give that firm effective control.

In spite of these very apparent problems, firms do enter joint ventures of this type. The motive of the multinational firm in such a situation is generally to take on a national identity and lower its profile with the local government. A local partner may join such a venture because it is attracted by the obvious expertise of the multinational and is unaware of the inherent conflicts in the situation, or perhaps because it believes it has found a way to side-step these problems. Two firms in this study entered such ventures as the local partner. In each case, the president of the firm was aware of the potential problems, but believed he had found a way to safeguard his company's position.

In one case, the joint venture plant was to sell the majority of its output to the multinational's marketing organisations in other countries, but a certain portion would be sold to the local partner at an attractive price, for resale in the local market. A low price was possible because of the high volume and specialised nature of the plant. Since the joint venture plant was the sole producer in the country in question, the local partner reasoned that it could soon gain a share of the local market and earn a substantial profit. The profitability of the joint venture itself was of little concern to the local partner. The only reason for entering the joint venture was to gain access to an excellent source of supply. Having mapped out its strategy in advance, this local company entered negotiations determined to take as *little* equity in the joint venture as possible. The equity contribution was viewed by the company as the price it had to pay to secure its source of supply.

The venture began well. The local partner was very satisfied to take only 30 per cent of a very small equity base in the joint venture, which was very highly leveraged. The bank debt was completely guaranteed by the multinational parent, as it wished to use bankers in its home country, rather than local banks. Although initially operating at a loss, the venture was earning a small profit within a year and performing better than expected. However, six months later, the profit turned to a loss as the multinational firm raised by 40 per cent its price on a substantial quantity of specialised material it sold to the venture. The local parent was not concerned, as it had profitably captured over 50 per cent of the local market. Its purchase price from the venture rose somewhat, but not enough to threaten the operation. For the next two years the venture operated at a loss, partly because of the increase in transfer price and partly because the volume in the plant was restricted by the need to keep other plants belonging to the multinational busy. Five years after the venture began transfer prices were raised again. The increase was 20 per cent on most components, but 90 per cent on those specifically used in the products sold to the local partner. (These products were slightly different from the rest of the line.) Although the executives of the local parent were never able to determine completely the reason for such a change (the stated reason was currency revaluation, which did not fit the facts), its effect was clear. The local partner could no longer compete in the local market.

At this point, the local partner pressed the multinational firm to buy out its 30 per cent equity position for the original cost. Executives of the multinational suggested that if the local partner wanted to leave the venture, it should pay its share of the cumulative losses (which were 10-15 times as large as the original equity position), as the net book value of the venture was negative, not positive. After some rather unpleasant negotiations, in which the fact that the local partner had signed no bank guarantees played a significant role, the local firm was able to recover its initial investment and the multinational took full ownership of the venture.

There is little doubt that the local partner was lucky to come out of this venture as well as it did. The firm had offered to sign a bank guarantee, provided local banks were used, but the multinational firm decided to use its own bankers elsewhere. The issue was not seen as particularly important at the time, in spite of the fact that the joint venture began life with a debt equity ratio of seventeen to one. In my opinion, the joint venture should never have been established in the first place. The product flows were such that it was an inappropriate place in the corporate structure for the multinational firm to involve a partner. Because of the product flows involved, *neither* parent particularly cared if the venture was profitable. Each could make money by selling to it or buying from it. Not until the break-up of the venture was the issue of the cumulative loss fully addressed. This theme will reappear. The major problem with heavy product flows is that they divert the attention of a joint venture's parents away from its performance, usually to its detriment.

The Economies of Scale Joint Venture

Joint venture to achieve economies of scale in production have long been used by steel companies in the establishment of coal and iron ore mines. By pooling their requirements, five or six companies can together create an economically viable mine. More recently, joint ventures have been formed in the automobile industry for the same purpose. Prevalent in Europe, particularly in companies such as Volvo, Peugeot and Renault, the trends seems to be spreading to North America in 1980. A joint venture is a method for smaller or weaker firms to combine engine or transmission plants, or in some cases dealerships (American Motors and Renault), to compete with the giants like General Motors and Toyota. This type of joint venture is also being used in the computer industry, by IBM's competitors. These smaller companies have joined in an effort to try and match IBM's economies of scale in the production and product development work of computer peripherals and components.

Any venture established to achieve economies of scale will involve product flows between the venture and its parents. A situation which led to the formation of such a venture in the computer industry is diagrammed in Figure 4.1 and discussed in some detail. Both the companies involved were large computer manufacturers, although small in comparison with IBM. IBM's superior economies of scale in production and particularly product development gave it a strong edge in the market.

As Figure 4.1 indicates, Divisions A1 and B1 both produced a

Figure 4.1: A Situation Leading to the Creation of an Economies of Scale Joint Venture

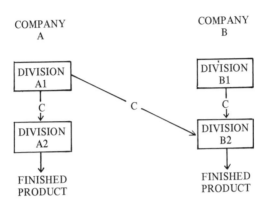

component C which was used by Divisions A2 and B2 to produce slightly different finished products. However, Division B2 also purchased some of its requirements for the component from Division A1, and this happened particularly when the component had undergone a recent design change. Although both Division A1 and B1 spent tens of millions of dollars annually on product modification and upgrading, A1 seemed to be superior in this regard. As a particular model of the component matured, Division B1 tended to catch up technically and B2 would increase its purchases from that source. However, a major modification typically came on the market every three years or so, just about the time B1 had caught up, and the cycle of purchasing from A1 began again.

In the 1970s, these two companies formed a joint venture to combine divisions A1 and B1. The venture continued to supply A2 and B2, but as a result of plant rationalisation it was expected to provide lower manufacturing overhead per unit, as well as lower product development costs per unit (the combined product development budget was cut by about 50 per cent) and, because of economies in purchasing and assembly, lower variable costs.

All of the output of this venture was to be sold to its parents, and this fact gave rise to some difficult problems. The transfer price between the venture and its parents was of principal concern. If the transfer price were set at a low level (as it was in this case), so that the joint venture would just break even, the economic benefit of the joint venture would reside entirely in the price of the component being shipped to its parents. Therefore, if the parents purchased the component in a proportion markedly different from that of their ownership percentages, the economic benefits of the venture would be unfairly distributed. If, for instance, company A contributed 60 per cent of the assets to the joint venture and held a 60 per cent ownership position, yet took only 40 per cent of its inexpensive output, it would be in a losing situation *vis-à-vis* company B, because the venture itself will produce no profit. Adjusting the ownership percentages of the venture to match the product flow could be a viable solution, but this could be difficult if the proportion of the flow going to each parent were not steady.

One solution to this problem is to raise the transfer price and capture the profit in the joint venture, whence it may be distributed to the parents in the appropriate proportions, but this may cause income tax problems. If the profit is created in the joint venture, it will definitely attract tax. However, if it is captured in the parent divisions it may be possible to write off other losses or deductions against it. The situation can become particularly complex if one parent has losses to offset against this benefit, whereas the other does not. In this particular example, the executives of company A were also concerned about the fact that they were losing the revenue they had previously earned selling the component to Division B2. Would the joint venture deal allow them to be compensated for this in some way?

It is clear that no matter where the transfer price is set, there will be problems. As a senior executive of the computer firm stated, 'in a joint venture of this type, there will always be a lot of problems, many of which you simply cannot anticipate. The key is to have such a large financial "carrot" (in this case the reduction of product development expenditures and the lower variable cost of the component) underlying the deal that each partner will try very hard to make the whole thing work.'

In spite of the parents' efforts, this joint venture did not work very well. Perhaps because the venture had a guaranteed market (its parents) the product design group lost touch with the real end market, who were the parents' customers who purchased the finished product. Instead of paying attention to this group, the joint venture personnel talked to employees of the parent firms to find out what product modifications they wanted. Unfortunately, the two parents could not agree on which way the market would go, and as a result the venture's product development group did very little. Gradually, the position of technical leadership, which Division A1 in particular had brought to the venture, was lost. Eventually, after eight years of declining performance, ownership positions were modified and one parent became dominant, and a clear direction for product modification was established.

The Local Distributor Joint Venture

In countries in which nationalism is on the increase, joint ventures are often created between multinational firms and their local distributors to serve the local market. Two of these ventures were included in this study. In each situation, a large North American firm had been exporting a product to a country which, concerned with its balance of payments and eager for more jobs at home, had pressed for local manufacturing by introducing tariffs and local content regulations. The choices facing the multinational were to do nothing and lose the market, set up a licence agreement or joint venture with a local firm or, if local regulations allowed it, set up a wholly owned subsidiary. The firms in this study favoured establishing a joint venture with the local distributor, as the distributor in each case had already proved himself capable of selling the product in the country and was already known to the multinational's managers. These joint ventures were simply assembly plants, assembling components shipped by the multinational and selling the completed product to the distributor's company for local resale. The product flows are shown in Figure 4.2.

Figure 4.2: The Local Distributor Joint Venture

In a situation like this, the foreign parent's profits will be determined by both the transfer price which it charges the joint venture for sub-assemblies and the profit of the joint venture. The profit of the local distributor will depend on the transfer price which it pays to the joint venture for the finished product and, as well, the profit of the joint venture. In such a system, the foreign parent will want a high price for its sub-assemblies and a high price charged to the distributor; whereas the distributor will prefer the opposite — a low price in each case. Possibilities for disagreement are great, particularly if the joint venture is unequally owned. If the venture is equally owned, the partners might agree to capture most of the profit in the venture and split it equally via dividends, but even this will be difficult as the foreign parent may face repatriation restrictions and withholding taxes if it tries to bring home dividends. Given the conflicting objectives of the parents, the most likely resolution in such a joint venture is a high transfer price paid to the foreign parent and a low one charged to the local parent, satisfying each firm's primary motivation but leaving little or no room for the joint venture to earn a profit.

One venture in this study, believed to be typical, was set up in this manner. The venture earned only 2 per cent on sales, which was not surprising, as its gross margin was only 8 per cent of sales. On the other hand, the distributor to whom most of the venture's output was sold earned a gross margin of more than 20 per cent. The only constraint on the transfer price practice of the parents was to create a 'decent looking balance sheet' for the joint venture since they wanted the venture to borrow some funds locally. An executive of the foreign parent explained his company's philosophy:

> We do not like to put too much capital in developing countries, so 20-25 per cent of a joint venture's equity is ideal for us. But whether we own 10 per cent or 51 per cent there are three things we must control — product quality, the decision to expand the company's equity base and any design directly related to the product's design or manufacture. This means that we always have a few of our own people in management positions in the venture.

This executive went on to explain that the company made its money by shipping parts to the venture and complied to the minimum acceptable extent with the country's gradually increasing local content requirements. When these go so high as to make the project uneconomic, the foreign parent would pull out its executives and attempt to sell its interest in the company to the local partner. A middle manager who had spent several years in the joint venture found it not so much a single company as two groups of people, each looking over the other's shoulder and doing everything possible to protect and promote the interests of its particular parent.

In a situation like this the joint venture's most important role is as a mechanism which allows companies with conflicting objectives to work together. It is not a profit maximising firm in the normal sense, nor does it contain a group of executives committed to a common goal. The longevity of such a venture is open to question, in part dependent upon local content regulations, which were at a 35 per cent level in the preceding example, and in part upon the ability of the parent companies to temper their antagonistic positions with a realisation of the mutual advantage gained through the joint venture. The basic weakness of such a joint venture stems from the flow of product between the venture and its parents.

For comparative purposes, it should be mentioned that this same foreign parent had a joint venture in a second developing country whose prospects appeared much more promising. In this case the local partner was not the distributor of the product and, consequently, the venture was free to sell to a variety of distributors for as high a price as it could manage. Since local content regulations were at 80 per cent when the venture was formed, there was never any question of the foreign parent supplying the venture; instead the emphasis was on developing local suppliers who could do the job efficiently and on expanding the joint venture to do more of its own work. The critical difference between this joint venture and the other is the lack of product flows between the parents and the venture. The attitude of the foreign parent is 'how can I help this venture grow?', rather than the defensive position of 'how can I maintain the profit level I used to make supplying goods to this country?' The local partner is an ally, essentially to success, rather than a rival, to be tolerated with suspicion.

Conclusion

There are times when shared management ventures must be used, and they can be used successfully, but there are also a great many situations in which shared management ventures are not necessary. So the first rule with respect to shared management ventures is to make sure you really need one. The next issue is design. The job of running a shared management venture is a very difficult one, as the next chapter will amply demonstrate, and, if the basic design features of the venture are not correct, the management job may be virtually impossible. The design features focused upon in this chapter have been partner selection, staffing and partner pay-offs, in particular the issue of product flows between the venture and its parents. The parents that get these issues right are well on their way to a successful shared management joint venture. All that remains is to manage it well!

Notes

1. The core skill concept was developed by Len Wrigley in his unpublished PhD thesis, 'Divisional Autonomy and Diversification', Harvard Business School.

2. Adler, Lee and Hlavacek, J.D., 'Joint Ventures for Product Innovation', study done for the American Management Association (Amacon, New York, 1976).

5 THE ART OF MANAGING SHARED JOINT VENTURES

The newly appointed general manager of a shared management joint venture will usually have very little in the way of guidelines or support systems to help him ease into his new job. Compare his position, for instance, with the new manager of a company division or wholly owned subsidiary. The division manager will be able to make use of well established parent company procedures for funds allocation and technology transfer. His reporting relationships and criteria for advancement are also likely to be well defined. In addition, the new division manager will probably have seen others before him doing the same or a very similar job, and if necessary he can get advice from peers in equivalent positions. The general manager of a shared management venture, on the other hand, is likely to find that he has to devise a means of creating a working relationship with two or more parents who have vague and possibly conflicting objectives, and, in this job, peers capable of giving useful advice are not abundant.

Although joint ventures, particularly shared management joint ventures, are not managed by any single individual, the venture's general manager is always close to the centre of things and thus is the focus of this chapter. The observations made in the chapter are based upon the problems and activities of the 37 managers in my study and upon observations made by Schaan concerning his sample of ten Mexican ventures. The chapter concentrates on those aspects of the manager's job which are unique to joint ventures, such as involvement in many ambiguous relationships and questions of allegiance, trust and autonomy.

Managing Ambiguous Relationships — Above and Below

Part of the complexity of the general manager's job is due to the wide range of ill-defined relationships in which he often finds himself. What would be a clear-cut, hierarchical relationship in a wholly owned subsidiary can be an uneasy bargaining situation in a shared management venture. The manager's relationship with his immediate functional subordinate is a good example of this. If these managers have

75

been provided by the venture's parents (and this was true in all but two of the 20 shared management venture's in my study), they very often will view their next promotion as coming from the parent, rather than the joint venture general manager. If the employee believes that his rewards and punishments are not controlled by the venture's general manager, that manager's authority will of course be limited. In practice, the situation is not often this clear-cut and the functional manager is generally not sure how much weight executives in his parent firm will give to evaluations of his performance made by the venture's general manager. This issue can become particularly intense if the general manager is proposing actions which the functional manager feels are not in his parent's best interest. Should he co-operate, and be highly thought of by the general manager, or balk and communicate directly with his parent?

The same degree of ambiguity can exist between the general manager and his superiors. In order to explore these relationships more fully I am going to discuss the case of Walter Kruger and the Baker–Amcoal joint venture in New York State. To preserve the company's anonymity both names and locations between Kruger and the parent company personnel have been disguised, but the important relationships have been preserved.

Walter Kruger was the second general manager of this venture, which had been established to sell capital equipment manufactured by the German parent, Baker Gmbh, in the US market. The venture was four years old when Walter took it over, and by that time many of the equipment's components were being manufactured in the US by Amcoal, the American parent, under licence from Baker. Both parents agreed that, in order to lower transportation costs and avoid tariffs, all manufacturing would be transferred to the US parent, once it proved itself capable of reading German levels of cost and quality.

Walter, himself a German, had been hired away from a British firm by Baker, given six months training in Germany, and then was sent to the US to manage the venture. His predecessor, Peter Schmidt, returned to the German parent and took up a new job, which included responsibility for the joint venture. In his new job Peter communicated with Walter about once a week via telex, telephone or letter. They discussed marketing strategy. Schmidt was closely aware of what the major competitors (most of whom were based in Europe) were doing and could relay and interpret this information for Walter. He was also sufficiently in tune with the United States market, having spent four years there, to realise the kinds of issues which Walter had to face.

Together, they made pricing decisions — discussing such things as whether or not it would be worthwhile to price low on a certain job, the first of a new type, in order to subsequently pick up other orders of the same type which they believed to be forthcoming. These pricing decisions were crucial, given the extremely competitive state of the United States market.

Walter's other important relationship was with Paul Bates, the executive Vice-President of Amcoal. Like Peter Schmidt, Paul was on the board of the joint venture and in frequent communication with Walter. In fact Paul's office was just down the hall from Walter's and they frequently discussed personnel issues, with Paul offering advice on US personnel practices. In fact Walter was not quite sure how much freedom he had in the selection of subordinates and at the time of this study he was concerned with the poor performance of a salesman who had been hired on the strong recommendation of the German parent. Walter was 'testing the water' to find out if he was free to deal with the man as he saw fit.

Through Paul Bates and Peter Schmidt Walter clearly had very close ties with *both* parents — not an unusual situation in a shared management venture. He observed that one of the most important tasks for a manager in his position was to decide who has to be involved in different types of decisions. He commented:

Decision making in a 50-50 joint venture can be rather confusing. Some decisions must involve both parents, others only one, and still others, I can make on my own. I try to recognize, in advance, which parent will be interested in each decision. For instance, the parents must decide between themselves whether subcontracted production is to take place here or in Germany. I present the relevant information, and may express an opinion, but the decision is theirs.

When we are making technical decisions, of course the German company wants to be involved; and in issues affecting relationships with US customers, we include the Americans. Fortunately, each parent recognizes the other's expertise, and the long-run viability of the joint venture is a strongly held mutual objective.

Sorting out the decision-making process was difficult, but something which could be learned over time. The greatest ambiguity which Walter faced appeared to be the role of Paul Bates. This issue arose because of the poor performance of Amcoal's division in Tennessee which was producing parts for the venture as a subcontractor. Walter was on the phone three or four times a week to this division enquiring about production schedules, product quality issues, choice of sub-vendors and, most frequently, price. It was Walter's contention, in early 1980, that this division, frustrated because it was not even covering full overheads on the manufacture of the equipment, was doing everything it could to recoup its losses through overpricing small parts and auxiliary equipment. 'They don't treat us as a real customer,' commented Walter, 'but rather as some kind of captive market'. He was taking his case, complete with documentation of the overpricing practices, to Paul Bates for resolution.

Walter's relationship with Paul Bates, however, had the potential to be an awkward one, as he was at the same time Walter's superior — as a representative of a major shareholder — and a member of a firm acting as Walter's supplier, in which capacity he should have been trying to please Walter. To make matters more complex, Walter was now asking him to act as an impartial arbitrator between Walter and the division manager. It is a situation like this that makes the management of joint ventures a difficult business!

Walter's relationship with Baker Gmbh also caused him some frustration. While Peter was very useful with respect to short-term pricing issues, Walter wanted to talk to someone about the long-term strategy of the venture. His week long trips to Germany never seemed enough to get this issue fully aired, and often the senior people he wanted to involve in such discussions were not available. What Walter may not have realised is that such uncertainty over objectives and strategy appears to be the norm in joint ventures. Schaan found that in only three of his ten Mexican ventures did the venture's general manager have a clear set of objectives that had been agreed to by both parents. In one of these three the process had been initiated at the joint venture rather than the parent level. I have quoted Schaan's description of the sequence of events, as it demonstrates nicely how a joint venture manager can manage his parents.

The need to develop an understanding of the parent's expectations and to create a clear set of criteria to measure the success of the venture arose after managers from the two parents had shown increasing concern that they did not understand what the venture was doing and where it was going . . . It was felt by some of the venture's top managers that what was needed was a concept of corporate strategy. When they started working at this task it quickly became apparent that other than profits they did not know what the expectations of the parents were . . . So they screened internal documents of both companies, annual reports, speeches by top executives of the two parents . . .

They came up with a set of hypotheses that they presented at the next board meeting. During that meeting managers from each parent commented on the list presented to them. They deleted some criteria, added new ones, reformulated or clarified others and the result of the discussion was that each party knew and understood what the expectations of the other two were. Some objectives were similar and others were divergent, so the next step taken by managers of the venture was to reconcile differences in order to come up with a list of objectives for the venture which reflected the interests of both partners.

A manager from the venture indicated that after this experience, the parents were very satisfied because they felt that they determined the corporate objectives of the joint venture.

A process like this does not take place very often. Schaan reported that seven of the ten venture managers in his study had in the past — or still had — difficulties in understanding the criteria of their two parents. This is not surprising since he also discovered that four of the parent companies did not know themselves how to judge the success of their venture, and managers of nine parent companies stated that there had been a period when they did not know or understand their partner's criteria of success.

A successful joint venture general manager has to have a very high tolerance for ambiguity, excellent negotiating skills and a good feel for what matters to each parent, because he may not be told explicitly. According to Schaan most venture managers' first goal is to avoid conflict and tension between their parents, only secondly do they try to achieve specific performance goals.

Allegiance

The lack of clarity which typically surrounds a joint venture's objectives and the fact that there is often a degree of conflict between the objectives of the venture's parents mean that the allegiance of the venture's general manager plays an important role in determining how the venture is run. Both parents and joint venture general managers see this issue of allegiance as very important. Walter Kruger volunteered the following statement regarding his own allegiance, stressing that his neutrality set him apart from most venture managers.

> My primary allegiance is to the joint venture, not to either of the parents. Of course, most joint venture managers would probably say that, but in my case it is true. The reason is that I did not have a permanent job in either parent company before coming to work here, and I do not particularly expect to be promoted into either of them if I leave this job. The fact that I was hired by the German parent and spent six months training in Germany offsets the fact that I am in more frequent contact with the Americans in my day-to-day job. After all, they are just across the hall. So I consider myself neutral; and, more importantly, I think both parents see me in the same way.

Schaan found that, even though he had not included allegiance on his interview guide, it was spontaneously raised as an important issue by the general managers of seven of the ten ventures which he was studying. One manager who, like Walter, was trying not to take sides with either parent was involved in a very complex situation. He had put forward an expansion plan for the venture which the foreign partner had said should be delayed for a couple of years because it was worried about a devaluation. As a result, the venture, which was at capacity, was going to have to decrease its exports (25 per cent of sales) in order to serve local Mexican customers. This was fine with the foreign parent who could serve these export customers from the US and earn 100 per cent of the profit in so doing. However the Mexican parent's viewpoint was totally different. This partner received a lot of goodwill from the Mexican government because of the joint venture's exports, and this was important because the price of the partner's own product on the Mexican market was totally controlled by the government. The venture was used as a 'flagship' company by the Mexican partner to indicate to the government that it was contributing to the achievement of the country's plan. Also, the joint venture itself received a number of grants and financing assistance because of its export programme, which would be lost if exports were eliminated. The joint venture general manager concluded that his position was extremely delicate, and he decided to try to arrive at a compromise which would enhance the position of the joint venture while doing the least damage to the aspirations of each parent. He put the joint venture's interests, as he perceived it, ahead of that of either parent.

It seems to be important that a venture general manager is free to take a 'neutral' or 'let's do what's best for the joint venture' approach to problems of this nature. In my study seven of the twenty shared management venture general managers were working for their venture on a part-time basis, in nearly every case because it was too small to support a full-time manager. Clearly, the allegiance of these seven managers lay with the local parent whose payroll they were still on. This should not be taken to mean that none of the other thirteen managers had a particular allegiance to either parent. Many of them did. One of the more spectacular examples that I saw of a strong bond between one parent and a joint venture general manager in a shared management venture (such bonds are common in dominant parent ventures) was in a large venture in California. The foreign parent in this venture was growing disgruntled with its continuing poor performance and decided to strike a task force (which did not include members from the local parent) to examine the situation. Included in the task force's mandate was an evaluation of the venture's general manager, who had been provided by the local parent. This manager was understandably concerned, but the local firm told him not to worry, they were not going to take the recommendations of the task force seriously anyway, the whole thing was a political exercise. In any case he was assured of a senior position in the parent company no matter how the dispute between the parents was resolved.

In order to try and get a feel for the allegiance of general managers beyond the simple categorisation of part-time or full-time employees, I asked whether or not they expected that in the future they would be working full-time for either of the parents. Twelve of the thirteen full-time managers answered this question, half of them indicating that there was a greater than 50 per cent probability that they would be working for one parent or the other when they left the joint venture. It seems reasonable to conclude that in these six cases the manager's allegiance would be with the parent company that he expected to join.

Thus only six of the twenty managers seemed free to play a neutral role in their venture, siding automatically with neither parent, examining each issue in terms of what seemed best for the venture. One distinct advantage to a manager of being tied to neither parent is that he has the opportunity to get a high degree of trust from both. A general manager is more likely to be left alone by a parent if he is considered to be an independent agent than he is if he is considered to be under the influence of the other parent. Being left alone can be very important, as the data in the following section indicate.

Trust, Autonomy, and Success

If you ask parent company personnel about the success of their joint ventures, in nine of ten answers the idea of trust will figure prominently. The following comment recorded by Schaan from a manager in a Mexican company which had been involved in 15 successful joint ventures is quite typical: 'So far, we have enjoyed very successful experiences with all our foreign partners. Profits and growth in an environment of *trust and mutual respect have been the golden rules of our relationships.*' (Emphasis added.)

I have always been rather sceptical of comments like this, because it seems to me that an environment of trust is something that develops, if at all, over time. If trust is more likely to be the result of success than its cause, it is not nearly as important as managers believe. Certainly one cannot advise a joint venture candidate to choose a partner he trusts. The advice would not be useful, because by the time one finds out if a partner is really trustworthy it is usually much too late to do anything about it. However, I have changed my views somewhat on this matter, partly because I now see a link between the autonomy of a general manager and the level of trust between the parents, and because I have identified what I call the failure cycle of joint ventures, in which autonomy and trust play an important role.

After listening to managers describe the demise of a number of shared management ventures, I have observed what seems to be a common pattern of decline and have labelled this the failure cycle. A typical scenario is that of a fairly young shared management venture in which performance begins to deteriorate somewhat, either against budget or against identifiable competitors. This decline may be due to a lack of competence on the part of the general manager, or it may be due to factors totally beyond his control. The parents are unlikely to be able to tell the difference and, in any case, the typical response is to monitor the venture's activities more closely. Review meetings may be held monthly instead of quarterly, and decisions will be reviewed in greater depth and detail than before. This intervention into the affairs of the joint venture, by two parents, is likely to slow and confuse the decision-making process. This in itself may cause performance to worsen further, encouraging the parents to become even more closely involved, so that the downward cycle will continue. This system

Figure 5.1: The Failure Cycle

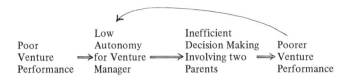

| Poor
Venture
Performance | $\Rightarrow$ | Low
Autonomy
for Venture
Manager | $\Longrightarrow$ | Inefficient
Decision Making
Involving two
Parents | $\Rightarrow$ | Poorer
Venture
Performance |

may not return to equilibrium, with the end result that what was initially a minor decline in performance can trigger a series of events leading to a major crisis. The cycle is illustrated in Figure 5.1.

Experienced shared management venture managers are aware of this cycle and stress that good early performance is an essential factor in the long-term success of a venture. One very successful manager who had been managing his venture for more than ten years explained that the first six months on the job were critical. If in that period a manager performed extremely well he could build a degree of trust that would stand him in good stead when the venture's performance, inevitably, did fall below expectation. If the manager is perceived as being good he may be able to keep the parents out of his domain, to let him solve the problem as he sees fit. Once both parents decide to 'help' the chance of solving the problem is greatly reduced. The other thing the manager must do in the first six months is demonstrate that he is an independent operator, not 'owned' by either parent. By doing this he helps to establish the parents' trust in one another, also reducing their interference. This line of argument suggests that some of the techniques of control which Schaan found in use in Mexico, and which were described in Chapter Two, are not appropriate for use in shared management ventures. The manager needs his freedom to act as he sees fit.

A second manager stated that his current joint venture had begun very badly and there was little doubt in his mind that without the trust created in an earlier venture the parents would have been 'all over him' in the first year and would probably have destroyed the venture completely. Thus trust is important because it leads to autonomy for the joint venture manager. These two managers made the automatic assumption that the more a joint venture manager is left alone, the better he will perform. My data, shown below, certainly support this contention, although there is some confusion between cause and effect here. I conclude that autonomy both results from good performance ('get off my back, I'm doing all right') and leads to improved performance,

Table 5.1: Shared Management Joint Ventures: Autonomy and Performance

(1) Managers' Perceptions

	FREEDOM TO MANAGE IS:		
	Less than it would be in a wholly owned subsidiary	About the same	Greater than it would be in a wholly owned subsidiary
Number of Ventures	6	2	9
Success Rate[b]	0%	50%	77%

(2) Autonomy Measured by Number of Decisions Manager Can Make on His Own[a]

	Low Autonomy (2 decisions or less)	Medium Autonomy (3–5 decisions)	High Autonomy[c] (6 or more decisions)
Number of Ventures	11	8	4
Success Rate[b]	36%	75%	100%

Notes: a. Managers were given a list of nine decisions and asked which type they made on their own, which with the involvement of the local parent, or foreign parent and which the parents made on their own. b. The success rate is the proportion of ventures not liquidated or reorganised due to poor performance. c. The ventures shown as 'high autonomy' were those classed as 'independent ventures' and are treated separately from shared management ventures in this study.

for the reasons stated earlier.

Table 5.1 indicates that there is a very strong relationship between autonomy and performance. Before leaving this subject it might be instructive to have a look into the life of a manager who is not given a high degree of autonomy by his parents. This is a much more painful situation than that of a manager not being given any autonomy in a wholly owned subsidiary. The potential for fighting and confusion and political intrigue increases enormously when two parents are involved. The manager quoted below ended up in hospital due to the stresses he incurred while trying to manage his venture.

This venture was performing poorly when I arrived, and I didn't know the business or the company. I had managed joint ventures before, but always in situations where one parent was clearly dominant. In this venture we had a management committee of 10 people; 5 from each parent, and they wanted to see and know everything. I spent 85 per cent of my time in the first year catering to the needs of the parents. Explaining how the joint venture worked, what it was doing, and why. The second year this may have fallen to 75 per cent but it never fell below 50 per cent. They discussed and debated *everything*. In no area was either parent willing to defer to the other's knowledge or expertise. I felt like I was dragging an elephant behind me whenever I tried to do something.

In the second year, I was able to get the management committee cut back to 6 people, but it really didn't make much difference since they were there primarily to funnel information back to the executives at head office. Both parents did this, and decision making was *very* slow. I also managed to get the 'untouchable' list, people I couldn't fire without permission of both parents, cut by about 50 per cent.

Of course not all general managers do not perform well when they are left alone, and conversely some managers enjoy a great deal of freedom even when they are not performing well. To stress the fact that preceding generalisations are just that, and that there are exceptions to each of them, the chapter will end with a quote from a manager whose predecessor was an exception to the norm. His comparison between managing a division for one of the parents and managing the venture is particularly interesting.

Before coming here I managed a division for one of the parent companies. I find the change in my job astonishing. In the division you have to go through a real inquisition to get funds, and budget reviews are no joke. This operation is about one quarter the size of the division with four times the freedom.

One reason I suppose is that the product line here is not closely related to that of either parent, but I think another factor is the make-up of the board. Very senior executives are on this board — guys who run the multi-million dollar parent companies. In comparison, we are tiny and thus get little attention, which is appropriate from their personal point of view, but the bottom line has been mediocre performance in this venture for years, of a type which would not be tolerated in either of the parent companies.

The directors are very polite with each other. Nobody really takes the gloves off the way they would if we were wholly owned. This may be due to the differences in personality between the firms. One parent is very tightly knit, with a lot of close personal ties between executives, all of whom live in a small town of perhaps 30,000 people. These managers tend to judge a man rather than a specific project. The other parent is impersonal, numbers oriented,

and prides itself on its discipline. They look at projects, not indivi-
duals.

*The net result is that this venture would probably have per-
formed better over the past ten years if it had been wholly owned
by either parent!*

Conclusion: The Role of Parents

If it was not clear already, reading this chapter would have convinced
any remaining sceptics that managing a shared management joint venture is a very difficult job. What also became clear in this chapter is
that many parent companies make the job more difficult than it needs
to be. It is not wise, for example, to try and ensure that the general
manager has a special allegiance to your firm ahead of that to your
partner, since by doing so you'll only earn the mistrust of the partner
and make the general manager's job more difficult. The best way to
ensure a healthy venture is to let the manager run it in what he feels
are the venture's best interests.

Even more difficult to follow, perhaps, is the advice that a parent
should not jump heavily into the affairs of a joint venture if it begins
to perform poorly. If both parents do get more heavily involved in the
joint venture's decision-making process it is likely to decrease, not
increase, the venture's prospects for survival. Giving a manager autonomy certainly does not guarantee success, but if both parents decide
not to give him any freedom, chances of failure are greatly increased.

6 OPTIONS FOR TECHNOLOGY-SEEKING FIRMS: JOINT VENTURES AS A MECHANISM FOR TECHNOLOGY TRANSFER[1]

Nearly every book which deals with the subject of joint ventures or licence agreements does so from the point of view of the firm which has technology and is wondering how best to exploit it. A great deal of attention has been devoted to exploring the trade-offs to be made between exporting, licensing, forming joint ventures and creating wholly owned subsidiaries. The local partner in a joint venture, or the licensee in a licence agreement, is always assumed to be waiting and available, ready to go along with whatever scheme the technology supplying firm has decided best suits its own interest. In the hope of partially rectifying this situation this chapter has been written for firms considering either joint ventures or licence agreements as a method of acquiring technical expertise.

In evaluating these two methods of acquiring technology, two factors seem important. One is the cost, to the technology-seeking firm, of acquiring technology using a licence agreement or a joint venture. The other factor is the effectiveness of the information transfer process between the two firms under each arrangement. In this chapter, two types of joint venture and two types of licence agreement are examined, and a set of guidelines is presented indicating where each of these four options should be used. Then, the actual practice of licensing and joint venture forming firms is compared with the guidelines. It does not spoil the punch-line to state now that licence agreements were used much as recommended, but joint ventures were not. An examination of the reasons for the unexpected joint venture behaviour led to new insights, and the chapter ends with some observations about the market for technology.

Licence Agreements as a Means of Technology Transfer

The major difference between licence agreements and joint ventures is that, in a licence agreement, there is no sharing of equity by the firms involved. All of the capital investment is made by the licensee, and the licensor simply agrees to provide technology, in exchange for a fee, which is usually a percentage of sales of the product in question. There are, however, two importantly different types of licence agreement. There are the *current technology agreement*, which gives the licensee access only to technology which is in existence at the time the licence agreement is signed, and the *current and future technology* agreement, which states that new development work done by the licensor in a specified product area during the life of the agreement, as well as current technology, will be transferred to the licensee. There are significant differences between these agreements both in cost to the licensee and in the process of technology transfer. A study which I did in 1975 indicated that the average contact time between licensor and licensee employees in future and current technology agreements was 45 man days per year.[2] This contact allows the employees of the two firms to get to know one another's strengths, weaknesses, and biases, and this tends to result in more efficient and effective information transfer. (Some evidence is given with respect to this in a subsequent discussion of information transfer in joint venture.) In licence agreements which provide only for the transfer of current technology, whatever contact there is between firms is typically during the first year of the agreement, and the sender and receiver of the information do not come to understand one another well.

Surprisingly, current and future technology licence agreements, which appear to offer more benefits to the licensee, do not carry higher royalty rates. I collected the following data from British licensees in 1976.

Further examination was carried out to see if royalty rates were a function of product age or of the uniqueness of the technology. They were not, thus raising the possibility that royalty rates may be simply a function of negotiating skills of the parties involved.

There are, however, other ways in which current and future technology licence agreements are more expensive for a licensee than current technology agreements. One of these is a restricted ability to export. As Table 6.2 shows, most Canadian licensees in the 1975 study with current and future technology agreements were not allowed by their licensors to export, whereas most with current technology agreements were allowed to do so. From the licensor's point of view, such restrictions make a great deal of sense. An American firm, for instance, which is supplying its latest technology to a Canadian licensee will want to have to compete in the US market with products produced by the Canadian licensee. The same type of reasoning leads licensees to restrict current and future technology agreements primarily to products

Table 6.1: Royalty Rate and Licence Agreement Type

Royalty Rate	Current Technology	Current and Future Technology	Total
Less than 2%	2	2	4
2–4.9%	6	9	15
5–10%	7	18	25
More than 10%	1	1	2
Total	16	30	46

Table 6.2: Export Restrictions and Product Age

	Allowed to Export[a]		Product Age[b] (years)		
	Yes	No	0–3	4–10	10+
Current Technology	18	6	20	4	3
Current and Future Technology	6	26	5	14	20
Total	24	32	25	18	23

Notes: a. The export statistics relate only to products manufactured by Canadian licensees. It is illegal for a licensor to restrict a British Licensee from exporting within the EEC. b. Product Age is the time in years between a product's first world introduction and its introduction by the licensee.
Source: J.P. Killing, 'Manufacturing Under Licence', *Business Quarterly*, Winter 1977.

which are more than three years old. As shown in Table 6.2, just over half of all current and future technology agreements were for products which had been on the licensor's market for at least ten years, with only 12 per cent being three years old or less. For current technology agreements, these proportions are sharply reversed, with more than 70 per cent of the products being three years old or less. The data are from the 1975 licensing study.

In summary, current and future technology agreements provide the opportunity for an effective transfer of information between licensor and licensee, but these agreements are restrictive, often prohibiting exports on the part of the licensee, and are usually offered only for older products.

Joint Ventures as a Means of Technology Transfer

There are two ways in which a technology-seeking firm can use a joint venture to extract technical information from a potential technology supplier. One is to form a dominant parent joint venture in which it is the dominant parent and the technology supplier is the passive parent; the other is to enter a shared management venture with the technology supplier.

In either type of venture, there appears to be greater motivation and opportunity for contact between technology supplier and technology receiver than there is in licence agreements. In 1977, for instance, a study was published comparing the use of joint ventures and licence agreements by British firms in India.[3] It was found that 78 per cent of the joint ventures' plants were constructed under the supervision of personnel from the technology supplying parent, whereas construction supervisors were only supplied by licensors in 26 per cent of the licence agreements. Transfers of plant level personnel occurred in 48 per cent of the joint ventures versus 15 per cent of the licence agreements.

In the study on which this book is based, there were five dominant parent ventures in which the technology-seeking firm took the dominant role, using the technology supplier as a passive partner. In two of these ventures, both involving simple technology, the transfer process was based solely on visits or phone calls, with no permanent personnel exchanges or loans, and was reminiscent of that in a licence agreement. However, in another venture an important technical manager was supplied by the passive parent on a full-time basis, and in another a large group of technicians were loaned by the passive parent to the venture for three months. Another reason that joint ventures offer a better opportunity for technology transfer than do licence agreements is that an executive of the technology supplying firm is typically on the board of directors of the venture. Thus, a joint venture engineer who is having difficulty capturing the attention of engineers in the technology supplying parent will often find that reminding these engineers that he has a direct line to their firm's executive on the venture's board will produce results. Licensees do not have such leverage over licensors.

The cost to the dominant parent of obtaining technology from a passive technology supplying firm can vary greatly. In one case in this study the technology supplier was given 20 per cent of the equity in the venture in exchange for its technology. In another the supplier paid cash for its 50 per cent share of the venture, but then received a royalty on sales as a repayment for its technology. The President of one Canadian firm using a dominant parent joint venture to extract technology from its partner argued that, on a cash flow basis, a dominant parent joint venture could be less expensive than a current and future technology agreement. He reasoned that in giving a technology supplier 20 per cent of the equity of the new venture in exchange for its technology, the cash (dividend payments) going to that parent would only be about 0.5 per cent of the sales. He based this calculation on after-tax earnings of approximately 5 per cent of sales, and a 50 per cent dividend payout ratio. This payment is far lower than most licence fees, and since it is payable at the discretion of the dominant parent it can be withheld until the venture is stable and profitable. The factor this President has not accounted for, of course, is that the technology supplier will own 20 per cent of the joint company, and this eventually could have a very high cost to the Canadian firm.

The other joint venture alternative open to a technology-seeking firm is to establish a shared management venture with a firm that has the needed technology. The major cost of such an option is that total control over the venture's destiny will not be possible, and that the decision-making process for the joint venture could be a real managerial headache, as outlined in earlier chapters. The probability of failure is much higher in a shared joint venture than a dominant parent venture. The benefit of using a shared management venture is that there is a possibility of very good technology transfer between the technology supplying parent and the joint venture. As documented earlier, the parents in a shared management joint venture nearly always assign personnel to the venture, provided that it is large enough to support a full-time management team. One clear example of the type of technology transfer which is possible when parent employees are assigned to a joint venture was provided by a British venture which was importing massive amounts of computer technology from the US. Within the venture were two Americans acting as senior staff whose only responsibility was to manage the technology transfer process. They communicated extensively with their former colleagues from the American parent, putting together detailed documents governing the transfer of technology. Both the US managers supplying the technology and the British managers receiving it had to sign the documents committing themselves to specific transfer timetables.

There were 13 shared management ventures in my study in which technology supplied by one parent was judged by the manager to be 'critical to the venture's success'. The general managers of each of these ventures were asked a series of questions about the process of information transfer from the parents to the venture. Questions such as: 'Do you get information when you need it?'; 'Are verbal comments

Table 6.3: Technology Transfer in Shared Management Ventures[a]

Effectiveness of Transfer	Yes		No		Total
	Daily/Weekly Contact with Tech. Parent	Monthly or Longer Contact with Tech. Parent	Daily/Weekly Contact with Tech. Parent	Monthly or Longer Contact with Tech. Parent	
60% or Worse	2	1	0	3	6
80% or Better	4	1	2	0	7
Total	6	2	2	3	13

Notes: a. These are shared management ventures in which technology coming from a parent was judged 'critical to the venture's survival'. b. Managers rated the effectiveness of the technology transfer process on a scale from 0% to 100%.

(and written documents) from the parent firm understandable?'; and finally, 'What is your assessment of the overall effectiveness of the information transfer process?' The responses general managers gave to the last question, with respect to their technology supplying parent, are given in Table 6.3.

Several interesting observations can be made from the data provided in Table 6.3. Six of the seven firms which rated the efficiency of their information transfer process at 80 per cent or above were in daily or weekly contact with their technology supplying parent, whereas this was only true for two of the six firms with lower effectiveness ratings. This is to be expected. More contact leads to a more effective transfer of information. Another observation is that ventures containing employees provided by the technology supplying parent were in contact with that parent more frequently than those which did not have such employees. One might have expected that, to the extent that the information required by the venture was in the head of the employee transferred to it, less contact with the parent would have been necessary. Although there are too few observations in Table 6.3 for significant conclusions to be drawn, they suggest that information transfer is more likely to be effective if employees provided by the firm sending the information are working for the venture receiving the information. It is easy enough to transfer hardware — blueprints, specification sheets, price lists and product samples — but real commitment on the part of the sender may be necessary to ensure the transmission of the intangible 'know-how' which is in the minds of those who use the hardware.

In summary, four options for obtaining technology have been discussed in order of increasing cost to the recipient, and in increase of opportunity for effective technology transfer. The current technology licence agreement involves little commitment on the part of the licensor to transfer technology well, but has the least cost to the firm receiving the technology as it seldom involves any restrictions. The current and future technology agreement is likely to involve more contact between the firms and a better process of information transfer, but it has a higher cost in terms of export restrictions and the age of available products. A dominant parent joint venture can have an even higher cost, in that equity is often given in exchange for technology, but the commitment on the part of the technology supplier will be commensurately higher. Finally, the shared management venture has the highest cost — a high probability of failure — but the best prospects for personnel transfer and the effective transfer of technology. The issue facing the technology-seeking firm is which of these options is more appropriate.

When Should Each Option be Used?

A set of guidelines has been created in this chapter to help firms choose among the four alternate methods of acquiring technology which have just been described. These guidelines are based on the following underlying proposition: the more a technology-seeking firm needs to learn about the business to which the new technology relates, the stronger the relationship it needs to form with the technology supplier.

If a firm is moving into an area of business about which it knows very little, it is going to need a good link with its technology supplier. However, as just discussed, gaining the commitment of a technology supplier and access to its personnel generally costs money, in one form or another, so one does not want to overdo it. The objective is to match the strength of the linkage with the task at hand.

Thus, in order to decide which of the four methods of gaining technology is most appropriate for it, a technology-seeking company must determine the extent of the learning job which it is setting for itself. Its need for learning will depend on the degree to which the firm is moving away from its established base of knowledge and skills. The further it moves away, the more learning will be required. For simplicity, it has been assumed in preparing Table 6.4 that the major areas of learning in relation to a new product are technical and marketing, and in each of these the skill needed for the product can be identical to existing skills, related to existing skills or unrelated to existing skills.

Table 6.4: Relationship Between Existing Skills and Those Required for the New Product

Technical Skills Required	Unrelated	Loosely Diversification	Related	Unrelated Diversification
	Related	Closely Related		Loosely Related
	Existing	Existing Business	Diversification	Diversification
		Existing	Related	Unrelated

Marketing skills required

Four strategies of diversification have been identified in Table 6.4. If the technology-seeking firm wants to become involved with a product which demands both technical and marketing skills unrelated to its existing skills, it will be undertaking *unrelated* diversification. *Loosely related* diversification is that in which only one of the two skills is unrelated to existing skills. *Closely related* diversification means that both the technical and marketing skills required for the new product already exist in the firm or are related to existing skills. The final category, *existing business*, is used to denote situations in which both the needed technical and marketing skills already exist in the firm. Figure 6.1 indicates the type of licence agreement or joint venture which a technology-seeking firm should use when diversifying. The Figure has been constructed on the principle that the greater the diversification the firm is undertaking, and hence the more learning it has to do, the stronger the link it needs with the technology-supplying firm.

Figure 6.1 also reflects the proposition that firms should be more conservative as the financial investment which they are making in their diversification rises. That is, if the diversification involves a small capital outlay, the firm might risk a less strong link with its technology supplier than would otherwise be prudent. Thus, in Figure 6.1 it is recommended that a firm planning a small-scale, closely-related diversification choose a current or current and future technology agreement, whereas a large-scale, closely-related diversification should be implemented via a current and future technology licence or a dominant parent joint venture.

The boundaries shown in Figure 6.1 between the four types of agreements are not intended to be exact. They have been constructed on the principle that, as a project increases in scale and degree of diversification, the necessary strength of relationship between parties

Figure 6.1: Diversification, Investment and Method of Technology Acquisition

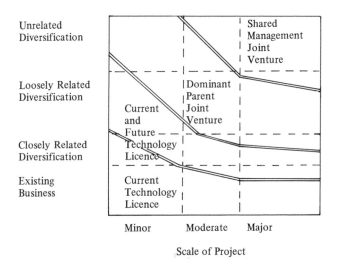

increases, and the type of agreement specified reflects this. Whether or not firms actually behave like this is a question addressed in the following sections.

Licensing Practice

Firms using licence agreements appear to behave much as expected. In the simplest situations — small or moderate diversification projects which make use of the firms' existing skills — only current technology agreements are used. In larger projects, and in less closely related diversification, current and future technology agreements are used much more often than current technology agreements. The information in Table 6.5, which allows these observations, was collected from Canadian and British firms in 1975.

The one major surprise is that some firms were using licence agreements to carry out unrelated diversification. It was expected that this would be done by joint venture (if not by merger or acquisition). Therefore a close examination was made of the licence agreements used in unrelated diversification situations. It was found that in the largest of these projects the licensees had taken unusual steps to increase the

Table 6.5: Use of Licence Agreements

	Investment ($000s)			
	<50	50–499	500 +	Totals
Unrelated	c = 0	c = 2	c = 0	c = 2
	c + f = 0	c + f = 0	c + f = 2	c + f = 2
Loosely Related	c = 1	c = 1	c = 0	c = 2
	c + f = 28	c + f = 2	c + f = 2	c + f = 32
Closely Related	c = 1	c = 4	c = 7	c = 12
	c + f = 3	c + f = 5	c + f = 2	c + f = 10
Existing Skills	c = 5	c = 6	c = 1	c = 12
	c + f = 0	c + f = 0	c + f = 2	c + f = 2
Totals	c = 7	c = 13	c = 8	c = 28
	c + f = 31	c + f = 7	c + f = 8	c + f = 46

Key: c = current technology agreement
     c + f = current and future technology agreement

strength of the bond with the licensor. In one case the licensee stipu-
lated that a senior executive of the licensor must come to work for
the Canadian firm for a period of two years, to be replaced by a fellow
worker when this term expired. This was the only one of the 74 agreements in which such a transaction took place. In the other large unrelated project the two companies were situated in immediately
adjacent cities on either side of the Canada–United States border.
Telephone communication between the firms took place, right down to
the level of draughtsman. Many problems were solved over a down-
town lunch. These examples, while apparently running counter to the
predictions made in Table 6.5, in fact strongly support the principles
on which it was constructed.

The Use of Joint Venture

There were 28 joint ventures in this study in which one firm was clearly
playing the role of technology supplier to the venture. As the information in Table 6.6 shows, these joint ventures were not used in the type
of situations which Table 6.5 had predicted. Shared joint ventures
were commonly used in situations in which it was expected that only
current and future technology agreements or dominant parent joint
ventures would be used. On the other hand, only one firm attempted
a large-scale, unrelated diversification using a shared-management
joint venture — the application for which it was predicted most shared

Table 6.6: Joint Venture Data

Diversification[a]	Investment ($000s)			
	<50	50–499	500 +	Totals
Unrelated	0	0	shared = 1 dominant = 0	shared = 1 dominant = 0
Loosely Related	shared = 1 dominant = 0	shared = 1 dominant = 0	shared = 1 dominant = 2	shared = 1 dominant = 2
Closely Related	shared = 2 dominant = 0	shared = 4 dominant = 0	shared = 5 dominant = 2	shared = 11 dominant = 2
Existing Product	0	0	shared = 1 dominant = 1	shared = 1 dominant = 1
Totals	shared = 3 dominant = 0	shared = 10 dominant = 0	shared = 10 dominant = 5	shared = 23 dominant = 5

Note: a. From the point of view of the technology-seeking firm.

ventures would be used. In short, technology-seeking firms seem to be getting involved in the complexity of shared management joint ventures in situations in which much simpler licence agreements or, at most, dominant-parent licence agreements should suffice.

This surprising result sent me back to the firms to find out why shared management ventures were being used instead of dominant parent ventures or licence agreements. The answer quickly became apparent: *many firms with valuable technology will only supply it to a joint venture in which they own 50 per cent and/or have a significant voice in its management.* Thus, the market for technology contains a significant discontinuity. Many technology-seeking firms try to set up joint ventures in which they will be dominant parent, but are offered only shared management deals. Faced with no other choice, or perhaps only the offer of an equally inappropriate current technology licence agreement, firms opt for the shared management venture. Better to get too much help from the technology supplier than not enough.

The Market for Technology

In the process of talking with managers of both technology dependent firms and technology suppliers, in an effort to understand the results in Table 6.6, a number of factors emerged concerning the market for technology. The overwhelming impression is of a small, fragmented, inconsistent market in which both buyers and sellers operate with little information. Several characteristics of the market which seem particularly relevant to managers of firms wishing to buy technology are discussed below.

The High Cost of Search

The major companies in an industry do not as a general rule, want to sell their technology. They might sell technology in a fringe area into which they ventured by chance, but they would usually rather capture for themselves the return on technology relating to their major businesses. This means that their preference is to serve a foreign market through exports or direct foreign investment, if the economics of the situation and the attitude of the foreign government involved will allow it. The implication for a potential technology purchaser is that it will have to look among the smaller firms in the industry and at firms in different industries to find willing technology suppliers. This does not result in an easy search process. It is made more difficult by the fact that many firms with good technology, which they would be willing to sell, do not consider the sale of information to be a particularly lucrative activity and, thus, do not advertise their positions, or even make it particularly easy for a buyer to negotiate a sale. They have more important things to worry about. Thus, the size and nature of the market is determined by the thoroughness and aggressiveness of the potential purchaser. The difficult decision which managers often face is whether to accept the deal they are currently being offered, which does not quite fit their needs, or to keep on with the search.

Disparate Choices

If a firm is persistent in its search for a supplier of technology, it may well end up with several very dissimilar offers for obtaining the same technology. In 1977 a Canadian firm was attempting a loosely related diversification of moderate scale — a situation which according to Figure 6.1 would call for a majority joint venture, or possibly a current and future technology agreement. However, one European firm offered the Canadians a current technology agreement with a royalty rate of 2-4 per cent of sales, while a second suggested a 50-50 joint venture in which the partner would supply machinery (rather than cash) as equity and would provide two executives for the joint venture. Neither choice was ideal, in the Canadians' view; one offering too much liaison with the technology supplier and the other not enough. However, because the firm felt it needed more help than was available with the current technology licence agreement, it chose the joint venture. A Canadian competitor subsequently picked up the licence agreement. Two years later the joint venture was liquidated, a victim in part of the lack of flexibility caused by having a partner thousands of miles away who needed to be consulted on decisions which the market demanded be made quickly. The competitor with the licence agreement has flourished.

The most difficult choice of supplier appears to arise in situations in which the quality of the technology varies between two suppliers, as well as the price and administrative mechanism (licence agreement or joint venture) demanded. A typical decision situation is that in which the firm with what appears to be the better technology will only supply to a 50-50 joint venture and demands a high price for it. The firm with the weaker technology is more flexible and offers a lower price. The buyer's indecision is often compounded by the fact that it is not completely confident of its assessment of the relative merits of the two technologies.

Price is Negotiable

Neither buyers nor sellers of technology seem to have a clear idea of the value of the commodity in which they are trading. A European firm recently asked to be given 40 per cent of the equity of a new North American joint venture to which it was supplying technology. The North American manager was not at all certain what the European technology was worth, but decided to make a counter offer of 15 per cent. The negotiation ended when both sides agreed on a final figure of 20 per cent. This reduction from 40 per cent to 20 per cent on the part of the technology supplier was very significant, as this was not a small joint venture. Another example of the uncertainty surrounding the price of technology was provided in the mid 1970s when a major US company was trying to attract partners into a joint venture in which it would supply the technology. The approach of this billion dollar company was to say, 'Here is the work we have done over the past ten years; what do you think it is worth?' At least one new entrant was astounded by this procedure, observing that if the creator of the technology could not put a value on it, how did they expect outsiders to do so?

Another sign of the confusion in the market is the previously discussed fact that current and future technology licence agreements, which appear to be more beneficial to the licensee, do not carry higher royalty rates.

Implications for Technology Buyers

Develop a Minimum Level of Technical Competence

To venture unprotected into an unstructured market like that just described is foolhardy. Even to function effectively as a technology buyer, a firm needs a certain technical expertise. Otherwise, it cannot begin to evaluate what it is being offered. Once a deal is signed, technical competence will again be useful in sorting out information coming from the technology supplier. One cannot simply accept uncritically all suggestions and technical specifications coming from a firm which may be a significantly different size from one's own and located in a different country. Many technology purchasers also find that transfer of technical ideas is much more effective if they have on staff someone who is trained in the relevant discipline and, thus, 'speaks the same language' as the engineer who is sending information from the supplying firm.

Know Your Needs

When shopping in a market as diverse and unpredictable as that for technology, a firm should have a very good idea of just what it needs in the way of help. Is marketing assistance needed, or just production process specifications? What about product design changes in coming years? Can the firm keep up-to-date on its own or will it need continuing help from the technology supplier? As stated above, the firm looking for technology is likely to be offered alternatives with radically different costs and implications. Unless a manager is very well aware of his firm's strengths and weaknesses, and in particular its ability to learn with and without help, these choices will be very difficult.

In addition to being able to size up his own firm, a manager should also be capable of assessing the character of a potential technology supplier. Is the firm used to transmitting its knowledge to others? Is it jealous of its technology or open with it? Will it be easy or difficult for the firm to gain the attention of employees of the technology supplier once a deal is made? As previously explained, a joint venture, with senior members of the technology supplier on its board, may readily get the attention of parent company managers and engineers, whereas the same may not be true if the only link between buyer and seller is a licence agreement.

Become Skilled in Shared Management Ventures

Most firms with valuable technology, if they are going to enter a joint venture at all, would prefer to be the dominant partner. They may, if they are very impressed with the apparent capabilities of their foreign partner, be willing to consider a shared management joint venture. Very few firms appear to be willing to supply important technology to a joint venture and play a passive role. (A separate study would be necessary to confirm this, but it is likely that it is primarily small firms that are willing to be passive technology suppliers, since they do not have the financial or managerial capabilities to participate in a shared management venture or to exploit their technology in the foreign country on their own.)

The author discovered a reluctance on the part of technology-seeking firms to enter shared management joint ventures. One reason for this aversion is that their potential difficulties are well known, and the tales of a few spectacular disasters are widespread. Less well known are the successes and the incredible benefits which can accrue to a firm which is in an equal partnership with a world leader in a particular technology. The effort made by many such technology suppliers to ensure that information is properly and completely transferred to the joint venture is equivalent to that which they would make for a wholly owned subsidiary. As described in Chapter Four, one leading German company spends $300,000 annually developing technology for and supplying it to a 50-50 joint venture in the United States. In addition, it has supplied two full-time managers to the venture, carries out training programmes for American personnel both in Germany and the US and, on a monthly basis, sends news of competitors, new product applications and tests of new products to the joint venture. In four years the venture's sales have doubled to $80 million. The problems of managing a shared management joint venture can be significant, but so can the rewards. Firms seriously interested in buying technology cannot afford a 'hands-off' attitude to these ventures.

Summary

Buying technology can be a viable corporate strategy; however, to use it effectively, a firm must have some minimum level of technical competence. The market is small and fragmented, and the deals which a technology-seeking firm uncovers will be largely the result of its own hard work. Firms with technology that they would be willing to sell seldom advertise the fact. When deciding whether or not to enter a particular deal, a manager should have estimated closely the amount of help he is going to need in the new product area and should also know the different degrees of access his employees will get to the supplier's personnel under various types of licence agreements and joint ventures. To be successful, a manager needs to know his firm's requirements and have the perseverance to locate a supplier who can meet them.

Many firms with technology will not enter joint ventures in which they own less than 50 per cent of the equity, and demand a managerial role. Thus, technology buyers may be faced with situations in which their only options are either a closer relationship with the technology supplier than they would ideally like or no deal at all. Firms that wish to pursue seriously a strategy of technology acquisition need to develop an expertise in the design and management of shared management joint ventures.

Notes

1. 'Technology Acquisition: License Agreement or Joint Venture?', *Columbia Journal of World Business*, Fall 1980.

2. J.P. Killing, 'Manufacturing under Licence', *Business Quarterly*, Winter 1977.

3. Howard Davies, 'Technology Transfer Through Commercial Transaction', *Journal of Industrial Economics*, December 1977.

7 BRINGING TECHNOLOGY TO NORTH AMERICA

This chapter brings together many of the issues discussed in the book, by recounting the history of two related joint ventures, each of which was designed to make use of European mining technology in North America. My original plan had been to use these very similar ventures to study the differences between joint venture success and failure, since one failed just prior to my study, while the other survived. This seemed particularly interesting since in each case the American partner was the same company, the products of each venture were sold to the same mining companies, and the European partners were both German firms with very good technology. However on close examination I decided that I was not dealing with one success and one failure, but rather one venture that had already failed and one which appeared to be on its way to failure.

On the surface, there seemed to be no reason that these ventures should not be successful. The products in question had been proven over a long period of time in European mines, and were just starting to be adopted by North American customers. The German partners were well established in the European market, and the American firm was of the largest distributors of equipment to US mines, and thus had good connections with many of the joint venture's potential customers. In spite of this, I have learned just prior to writing this chapter that the second venture has also collapsed, making both of them failures. In Chapter Five, using disguised names and locations, I described the job of Walter Kruger, the general manager of one of these ventures. The same disguise has been continued in this chapter.

The Baker–Amcoal Joint Venture

In 1969 the American Coal Machinery Company (Amcoal) of Cincinnati formed a very modest 50-50 joint venture with Baker Gmbh of Frankfurt, Germany. The purpose of this venture was to import Baker's hydraulic roof supports, a produt used in the longwall method of mining coal, and to promote their sale in the United States market. Although each firm contributed only $50,000 in equity to the venture and it was only to have one employee initially, it was an important move for both partners as it gave them a foothold into the US longwall mining equipment market. To appreciate the significance of this, it is necessary to understand a little of the business of mining coal.

Underground coal mining was, historically, a very labour-intensive process. However, in the late 1940s a new piece of equipment known as the continuous miner was introduced in the United States. This machine broke down the coal face and dropped the coal onto a conveyor system, eliminating the halting and sequential drilling and blasting process used previously. In Europe, a different system of automation was introduced, known as longwall mining. This involved three pieces of specialised equipment: a roof support system, a shearing machine (for slicing coal from the coal face) and a heavy-duty conveyor system. The roof supports made this system very safe, and thus especially appropriate for deeper mines. Overall, the longwall system offered very high output but required a substantial capital investment on the part of the mining company.

Amcoal's desire to form a relationship with a European manufacturer of longwall equipment was based on the fact that, since the early 1960s, it had been widely predicted that the United States' mining industry would adopt the longwall mining system. Mines were going deeper, safety was becoming a more pressing issue and hourly labour rates were rising. Amcoal, although a significant manufacturer of continuous miners, knew nothing of longwall technology.

Baker's search for a joint venture partner was the result of an earlier attempt to enter the US market on its own. In 1966, the German firm had sent a salesman to New York to 'spearhead' the firm's entry into the US market for roof supports. This was a considerable act of faith, as the first ever order for roof supports in the United States had only been placed a few years earlier, and Baker had an almost insignificant market share of the roof support business even in its own country. Not surprisingly, this lone salesman from an almost unknown German firm selling one component of a new and expensive system of mining met with significant difficulties. Customers wanted to see a permanent commitment by the German firm in the United States. Where were its warehouses? Where were the technicians who would service the equipment? The Germans replied that the investment would be made once the orders were in hand, but the Americans suggested that the sequence be reversed.

After three years of frustration, and no sales, this man recommended that Baker form a joint venture with one of the leading American mining machinery firms. Such a venture would give them both the needed credibility and, it was hoped, solid access at high level to the customers whom he had thus far wooed in vain. A report accompanying the recommendation suggested that the American market for longwall mining equipment was just about to take off.

Thus, the joint venture was formed, and Baker assigned a technical sales expert to Cincinatti, to become the venture's only employee. At the same time, Amcoal created a new position in its own hierarchy: Vice-President of longwall sales; and this man, and the German technical expert began a seemingly endless round of calls on American mining firms. It quickly became apparent that the potential American customers, being very unsure of themselves in this new technology, would demand a package deal — roof supports, conveyor, and shearing machine — which would perform properly as a single unit. They did not have the sophistication to design their own systems and buy equipment from each manufacturer separately. Accordingly, the joint venture made arrangements with suppliers of conveyors and shearing machines so that it could put together a total package — about a $3 million purchase for a customer at that time.

In spite of these efforts, it was a full two years before the first American order for Baker roof supports was obtained. This order was placed after the direct intervention of the President of Amcoal, who knew personally the President of the buying firm. Incredibly, particularly from the point of view of Baker, a company which had been working for six years toward this sale, the equipment performed very poorly. The problem was not with Baker's roof supports but with the shearing machine, supplied by a British firm as part of the package. Finally, this machine was removed from the mine and replaced with a Kohmag shearing machine ('the Cadillac of the industry') from Germany. Due to the heroic efforts in the field of the joint venture's technical man, a good relationship with the customer was maintained and the installation was eventually brought up to operating standards.

The roof supports to fill this order were manufactured completely by Baker in Germany and transferred to the joint venture at a price just high enough to allow Bake to cover its variable costs and overheads, with no allowance for profit. The principle established between the partners was that the profit on the product would be captured within the joint venture, so that it would be shared equally. This meant that the relative pay-offs between the partners did not depend on who was doing the manufacturing — and it would not matter if the manufacturing job were shifted from one parent to the other. The full set of pay-offs, previously listed in Chapter Two, are reported in Table 7.1.

Table 7.1: Amcoal Monetary Benefits to Parents

To Baker Gmbh	To American Coal Corporation
1. 50% of all dividends	1. 50% of all dividends
2. an engineering fee based on joint venture selling prices: (a) 7% if Baker had to perform prototype design and testing (b) 5% if some engineering was required, but no testing (c) 3% if no engineering was required	2. 3% of cost of goods sold in recompense for sales leads 3. a warehousing fee, to compensate Amcoal for the space taken in its warehouses by longwall parts 4. an administrative fee in return for administrative services performed for the joint venture
3. coverage of overhead in addition to variable cost on parts manufactured for the joint venture	5. coverage of overhead in addition to variable cost on parts manufactured for the joint venture

This list requires some explanation. Amcoal's 16-man salesforce referred potential longwall customers to the joint venture and for this Amcoal received a fee of 3 per cent of the cost of goods sold for the venture. The joint venture office was located within the Amcoal complex and many overheads and services were shared. The administrative fee mentioned in Table 7.1 was simply the venture's share of those expenses. The same was true of the warehousing fee.

In 1970 Baker developed a superior new type of shielded roof support and as a result made significant inroads into the German market. By 1974 the surprising US resistance to this breakthrough was finally overcome, again with the personal assistance of the President of Amcoal, who virtually personally guaranteed a close friend who ran a major coal company that the new product could perform better than anything else he could buy. This time, with a Kohmag shearing machine as part of the package, it did.

This installation proved to be the break that was needed to crack the US market. Between 1974 and 1977 twenty installations were sold, including one which set a world record for coal production in a 24-hour period. During this period approximately $400,000 in earnings were distributed to each parent and enthusiasm for the joint venture ran high.

Baker's European competitors were not asleep, however, and by 1977, pretty well every firm had its own version of the Baker shielded roof support and were fighting hard to recapture lost market share. In the United States in particular firms seemed to be pricing at and below cost in order to have at least one system installed and operating which they could use as a showpiece when the long-awaited market boom arrived. There were no fewer than 15 firms competing for the as yet small market. No one wanted to leave just when the party might begin, even though it was already ten years later than predicted. As a result of this intense competition, the joint venture sold only one set of roof supports in 1978.

This dismal sales performance prompted an evaluation of the partnership by senior management in both Baker and Amcoal. It was concluded that the joint venture needed to have its own technical and sales people who could concentrate solely on longwall sales. The American parent's salesforce was simply not trained to sell the new equipment, and the one competent man from Germany could not cope with the whole of the United States market. In the autumn of 1978 the company was reorganised. A new technical man was hired by Baker in Germany, given six months' training in the product and its applications and then sent to the United States to work for the joint venture. Several salesmen were hired from outside the firm. The sales manager and administration manager came from Amcoal, as Amcoal did many of the accounting and miscellaneous administrative chores for the venture. Parts and service employees would also come from Amcoal – in jobs which they had already been doing as part of the warehousing service which Amcoal had been performing to support longwall sales. Total employment would number approximately 15, under the direction of Walter Kruger, the new general manager.

As a further part of this restructuring, each parent contributed additional equity of $200,000 to the venture. While the reorganisation was taking place, Amcoal was becoming more involved in the production of roof supports. Three reasons underlay the decision to shift production of roof supports to a US division of Amcoal. These were: (i) some of the joint venture's customers were mines owned by steel companies, and they wanted the roof supports to contain American steel; (ii) as competitors caught up with Baker's product design lead, price became more important, and the freight and tariff involved in shipping the finished product from Germany were high; and (iii) Amcoal needed the work, as some of its plants were below capacity. Even though the transfer price was set so that Amcoal would not earn a profit selling to the joint venture, the overhead coverage would be very useful. In 1976 transfer of manufacturing information had been initiated, although all the product was still supplied from Germany. In 1977 Amcoal manufactured about 50 per cent of all units, and by 1979 completed units were no longer shipped from Germany, although Baker still supplied the hydraulic components.

Unfortunately, the cost performance of the division of Amcoal which was manufacturing the roof supports was well above expectations. The division could not match the landed cost of units imported from Germany and cover its normal overheads. In the interests of equity to the German partner, however, it was decided that Amcoal would supply product at the equivalent of the German landed price. The high cost of US production did not seem to be related to problems of technology transfer from the Germans. Baker Gmbh routinely used local German subcontractors for up to two-thirds of its production and thus was used to telling other people how to make their products. The manufacturing job taken on by the Americans was not in fact technically complex and a series of visits in both directions across the Atlantic seemed sufficient to get US production up and going. Nor was there resentment on the part of the Germans on account of the fact that the Americans were taking on the work, as it reduced the amount which they subcontracted out, not their own workload. Baker was very busy at this time producing roof supports for mines in Poland and China.

There was considerable debate about precisely why the US costs were higher than those in Germany. Walter Kruger and Baker executives stated flatly that it was simply because it took the Americans more hours to build the equipment. Walter explained that this was due at least in part to the fact that there was not much work in the Amcoal diision doing the manufacturing and thus the workers tried to stretch it out to delay the inevitable lay-offs. However, the executive Vice-President of Amcoal felt that the hours in the US plant were as low as those in Germany but that the American steel was more expensive than that in Europe, and this caused the cost differential. No one disputed the fact that the Amcoal division manager involved wanted to get rid of the joint venture work as soon as he could find something to replace it with. As a profit centre manager, he was not delighted to being given a job to do which by definition was intended to provide him with no profit.

The fundamental question raised by this case history is whether the manufacturing function should have been transferred, not from the German parent to the American parent, but from the German parent to the joint venture itself. The arrangements governing the transfer of product from the German parent to the venture appeared to be very well done, and this situation did not give rise to any international problems. The transfer price was clearly and openly established, and the decision to capture profit in the joint venture rather than in the German parent seems sensible. The major impetus for altering the situation was the increased importance of the transport and tariff costs incurred in shipping the product from Germany. Problems began to develop between the parents as it became apparent that the product could not be produced as cheaply in the US as it had been in Germany. These problems highlight the fact that there might have been significant advantages to moving the production to the venture, rather than the US parent. For instance:

1. The low transfer price between Amcoal and the joint venture meant that the Amcoal division manager was not motivated to perform well. Producing goods for the joint venture did little to help his profit and loss statement. If the manufacturing work had been done within the joint venture, the motivation of the man in charge would presumably have been at a much higher level, and lower variable costs would probably have resulted.

2. If the manufacturing function had been in the joint venture, it is likely that more personnel from the German parent would have been involved in it. Communication between the manufacturing operation in the US and that in Germany would have been much more extensive. The usual practice in such a situation is to second employees to the venture on a rotating basis. Had the manufacturing been done in the joint venture, any problems would have belonged to *both* parents, not just one.

In 1981 Amcoal sold its 50 per cent interest in this venture to Baker, citing low margins, high working capital needs of the business and low priced foreign steel as the reasons for the sale. Its demise will be compared with that of Kohmag Amcoal at the end of the chapter.

The Kohmag-Amcoal Joint Venture

The Kohmag-Amcoal joint venture was formed in 1976. Like Amcoal's earlier venture with Baker, it was a 50-50 deal, and Amcoal's intention was again to strengthen its longwall product line. In this case the product, the Kohmag shearing machine, was particularly attractive, as it was generally considered the finest product of its type in the world, and its market share in the United States was well over 50 per cent. Amcoal executives felt that by manufacturing Kohmag shearing machines in its Tennessee division, which was part of the plan, Amcoal's own production expertise would be upgraded to German standards.

Kohmag–Amcoal was Kohmag's second attempt to form a joint venture in the United States. In 1964 the German company had formed a venture with one of the largest producers of mining equipment in the United States, in order to have the American firm manufacture Kohmag shearing machines under subcontract to the joint venture, whch would sell them. Initially, the machines would be imported from Germany. Although the marketing aspect of this venture was successful, the programme to establish an American manufacturing site was not. According to one observer, there was a great difference of philosophy between the partners: 'The American parent looks at a market, decides what they can charge, and then figures out how to build a product to meet the price. The Germans build the product the way they think it should be built, no compromises, and then charge whatever is necessary.' This philosophical difference led to disputes between the partners, with the Americans continually wanting to loosen the tolerances to which Kohmag worked. Eventually the Americans began to develop their own line of longwall equipment even while selling the German equipment. In 1973 the joint venture was dissolved, and the Americans' new shearing machine came on the market at a price 50 per cent below that of the Kohmag machine, but it performed very poorly and by the end of 1975 only three units had been sold.

After the break-up of this joint venture, Kohmag formed a wholly owned subsidiary, Kohmag America, built around a nucleus of seven company employees who had earlier been sent from Germany to the joint venture. Since Kohmag, a relatively small family-owned company, was reluctant to invest in manufacturing facilities in the United States, it was decided that the subsidiary would simply import the product from Germany until another solution could be found. A deal was made with Amcoal, which had an extensive set of warehouses in the coal-mining regions of the United States, to perform the warehousing and delivery functions for Kohmag America. In spite of the excellence of its equipment, Kohmag was worried by the high price of its product and was anxious to find a way to begin to manufacture in the United States.

After three years of a very successful warehousing agreement, a deal was struck between the President of Amcoal and the senior patriarch of the Kohmag family. Amcoal would purchase 50 per cent of Kohmag America for $1.5 million and would make the capital investment necessary to begin production of Kohmag shearing machines in its Tennessee division. Initially, all machines would be imported from Germany (at Kohmag's list price, less 10 per cent) but as quickly as

Table 7.2: Kohmag-Amcoal: Monetary Benefits to Parents

To Kohmag	To Amcoal
1. 50% of all dividends	1. 50% of all dividends
2. a licence fee of 9% of the price to the end customer of all goods manufactured by Amcoal and sold to the joint venture	2. a 3% of all venture sales "participation fee" in recompense for sales leads
3. full profit less 10% on all goods shipped to the joint venture	3. an administrative and warehousing fee
	4. a 10% profit on parts manufactured for the joint venture

possible these imports would be replaced with goods of Amcoal manufacture. One condition of the deal was that Kohmag would be in strict control of all product engineering. It was anticipated that the joint venture would have a gross margin between 30 and 40 per cent once production was done in the United States. A complete list of the monetary benefits designed to flow to each parent is given in Table 7.2.

The creation of the joint venture was not greeted with enthusiasm by the employees of Kohmag America. They had been doing well in the US market and suspected that the manufacture of their products by Amcoal would cause headaches and confusion. The general manager was used to making his own personnel and pricing decisions and saw no reason to change just because Amcoal had purchased half of his company. This was unlikely in any case, as no Amcoal employees joined the new venture, except three who joined the Board of Directors which met only twice yearly. There was very little contact between anyone at Amcoal and the joint venture, except at the engineering level. The general manager occasionally sought help with high-level sales leads, but this was not frequent. Although I arrived too late to include this venture in my sample and did not get to talk to the man who was general manager for most of the venture's life, it seems likely that Kohmag-Amcoal would have been categorised as an independent joint venture.

If there was little communication between the venture and its American parent, there was even less between the parent themselves. Amcoal seemed reluctant to break in on an established relationship between the German company and its former daughter company, whereas the Germans seemed to hope that the Americans, being located in the same city as the venture, would actively monitor the venture's activities for them. One illustrative incident involved a senior manager in the joint venture whom neither parent thought was doing a good job. Twelve months passed before the subject was even discussed between them. The Americans had concluded that, since the Germans had hired the man, they must be happy with him, and the Germans felt that the Americans must find him acceptable as they saw him in action more frequently (they thought) and never raised any objections. The man was eventually fired. Another apparent communications problem was that decisions made by the board concerning the manufacturing of the product were seemingly never communicated to the manufacturing division. The general lack of communication, particularly between the parents, resulted in a very great deal of freedom of action for the general manager of the joint venture, so he made no move to alter the situation.

In what was described by one observer as a 'major act of faith that the longwall market would develop', Amcoal invested $8 million to expand its Tennessee plant, in part so that it could build Kohmag shearing machines. However, in spite of the fact that a German technical man from the joint venture, was posted full-time in the Tennessee plant, the transfer of technology from Germany posed some problems. These were accentuated by the fact that the technology itself was very complex – much more so than that involved in the construction of Baker roof supports – and that the drawings and materials lists were in German and in metric measurements. In addition, the engineering employees of Kohmag in Germany had never before had a set of their drawings leave the company and were very possessive of their technology, realising its importance to the overall success of their company. They never told the Americans any more than was necessary, and often less.

Communication between American engineers in Tennessee and the Germans in Hamburg was very distorted, as the Germans preferred to deal only with the engineering managers in the joint venture whom they already knew, rather than with the American end users of their information. A final complicating factor was that much of the work on the Kohmag shearing machine was done for Amcoal's Tennessee division by subcontractors. This meant that not only did Amcoal itself have to interpret drawings and instructions, but it also then had to explain these to third parties. The subcontractors considered this very undesirable and overly complex work and charged accordingly.

As a result of these factors, production in the United States began very slowly. In the opinion of one American executive, it took Amcoal three years to get to a position they should have been in after six months. Several further factors became clear as time passed. One was that the attitude within Amcoal, which the President wanted to upgrade through exposure to German manufacturing standards, was deeply ingrained. One particularly expensive example involved $400,000 worth of gears which a supplier delivered to Amcoal in Tennessee. The whole shipment was refused by the German technical man in the plant for being not within the tolerances demanded. Subsequently, an Amcoal employee accepted the shipment as being 'close enough'. When the German parent discovered this, Amcoal itself had to pay for the gears and they were not used in Kohmag shearing machines. It also appeared that the Germans were very serious about maintaining engineering control over the product. Questions of simplifying the production process were repeatedly raised at the board level by the Americans but the Germans would tolerate no changes. In addition, American costs were going to be higher than anticipated and, in fact, it would be a struggle to meet Kohmag's landed price from Germany. In the German's view the reason for this was that Amcoal was not sufficiently vertically integrated. It farmed too much work to suppliers, each of whom made a profit on the transaction. In Germany, Kohmag's plants were self-contained to the point that the firm did its own castings, machining and gear cutting. Amcoal resisted making the large capital investment necessary to bring such operations in house, arguing that the market was not big enough to justify such a commitment. One Amcoal executive commented sadly, 'they will never be happy until we have built a plant here which is a miniature of what they have in Germany'.

By 1978, the venture was clearly not developing as expected. The fact that Amcoal was only producing about 20 per cent of the parts required by the venture and was doing so at high cost, severely distorted the pay-offs which the parents had expected to receive. The gross margin was nowhere near the planned 30–40 per cent, due both to the high costs of importing from Germany and purchasing from Amcoal as a subcontractor. Because there was little profit, other forms of pay-off became very important. For instance, in one three-month period in 1978, Amcoal received a three per cent of sales participation fee of $98,000 and a warehousing fee of $90,000. However, Amcoal's share of profits for the whole year was just over $5,000. Kohmag, it may be recalled, was to receive a nine per cent fee based on the value of work done under subcontract by Amcoal. This, however, amounted to virtually nothing, as Amcoal produced so little. In terms of fees taken from the venture, Amcoal was clearly far in advance of Kohmag. However, the great unkown factor, and one on which the Germans refused to enlighten the Americans, was the amount of profit made by Kohmag on its shipments of shearing machines and parts to the venture. Amcoal executives suspected that the figure was substantial.

In 1979 executives from Amcoal and Kohmag mutually agreed to end the joint venture, and Amcoal sold its 50 per cent interest in the company back to Kohmag. The agreement by which Amcoal had carried out warehousing and delivery of Kohmag equipment before the venture was formed was successfully reinstated. Senior executives from Amcoal and Kohmag jointly visited major customers to inform them that the parting had been amicable and to assure them that quality, delivery and service on Kohmag machinery would not suffer – which it did not. Under a new general manager appointed by the parents six months before the collapse of the venture, sales rose from 10 units in 1978 (a 50 per cent market share), to 15 in 1979 (66 per cent market share) and were forecasted at 22 for 1980 (80 per cent market share). The new manager stated that life was 'much simpler' managing a wholly owned subsidiary and he was relieved not to have the constant production problems with Amcoal to worry about. In early 1980, together with executives from Kohmag, he was looking for a site on which to build, at long last, a wholly owned US manufacturing facility.

A Comparative Analysis: Why Did These Ventures Fail?

The demise of these ventures was not a result of the way they were managed. Although Baker–Amcoal was a shared management venture, this had little, if anything, to do with its problems. Kohmag–Amcoal was, on the other hand, an independent venture, and according to my findings this should have maximised its chances of success. What, then, was the problem?

I believe that the critical factor leading to the failure of each of these ventures was their underlying design. When the manufacturing function was shifted to North America from Germany, it should have been taken over by the joint venture, not the parent company. Moving production to the parent created unhealthy patterns of pay-offs and penalties between the parents, poor technology transfer in one venture, transfer price problems and, as documented in Chapter Five, all of this made life extremely difficult for the joint venture general manager. I have already detailed several explicit advantages that would have accrued if production had been moved into the Baker joint venture, and the discussion below is a similar analysis of the Kohmag venture. The problems in the Kohmag venture, both before and after the shift of production to North America, were more severe than those in the Baker venture.

Throughout the life of the Kohmag venture, the transfer price governing the shipments of goods from Germany to US was an irritant, because the Americans did not know how much the Germans were making on these transhipments. Their suspicions, heightened by their own problems, were that the Germans were making plenty. Whether this was the case or not, the lack of trust created by the Germans' secrecy was a serious problem. Compounding this problem was the fact that even by 1979 Amcoal's Tennessee division was capable of producing only half of the components of a Kohmag shearing machine and could do so at a cost only marginally better than the landed cost of equipment shipped from Germany to Kohmag at list less ten per cent. It had been expected that Amcoal would be able to do 90 per cent of the manufacturing by this time, at costs at least 30 per cent lower than those from Germany. The effect of Amcoal's poor performance was felt particularly keenly by the Germans. They lost the profit that they had formerly made on the 50 per cent of the production which was now manufactured by Amcoal, but, because of Amcoal's high costs, they were not rewarded by profits flowing back from the venture. Amcoal was not any happier, producing a product on which they were making no money and paying a nine per cent licence fee to the Germans to do so. One of the reasons for the poor performance was the inherent complexity of the Kohmag technology but, as in the Baker venture, other problems might have been alleviated, had production been shifted to the venture instead of the parent.

1. The technology transfer process between the engineers in Hamburg and those in Tennessee was exceptionally ineffective and inefficient, as all information had been relayed through the joint venture — through German personnel, with whom, presumably, the Hamburg engineers felt comfortable. Had the production taken place in the joint venture at least one step in this process would have been avoided, and perhaps engineers would have come from Hamburg to join the venture.
2. Only a single German was posted to the Tennessee plant, hardly a sufficient action to instill in the American workforce the concept and demands of close tolerance production as practised

by Kohmag. The acceptance of the off-tolerance gears by US personnel showed how little effect the Germans had. Again, if the production had been in the joint venture, the German production culture would have been more strongly represented.

3. The US division manager, who was paid on the basis of the profit earned by his division, was asked to transfer output to the joint venture at cost plus ten per cent and to increase his production of that product as quickly as possible. Clearly he was not enthusiastic about the situation. As in the Baker case, this unhealthy situation could have been avoided by manufacturing in the joint venture.

4. One of the reasons the US division's costs were too high — and the Germans were very insistent on this — was that they made extensive use of subcontractors. Kohmag executives constantly urged the Americans to make a greater investment in machinery and equipment to bring these jobs in house. Amcoal, alone, was not willing to make the investment. Had the manufacturing function been jointly owned, and thus the new investment shared between the partners, it might have been made.

These arguments seem persuasive, and at least after the fact, quite obvious. Why, then, did both ventures choose to have manufacturing done by the North American parent? Company executives responded that the investment required in new facilities would have been too great for the joint venture to bear. The parents were also not sure when the market would develop, and complained of exceptionally stiff competition. In addition it did not seem to make sense to build new plants when Amcoal had both space and labour available. In my view, however, there was another major factor involved, and that was that the parents were not sure of each other. Each was not convinced that the other had the necessary skill and drive to make a success of a major investment. Combining the risk that the market might not develop with the risk that the partnership might not work proved too great a hurdle. I find it significant that, once free of the venture, Kohmag decided to go ahead with the investment on its own.

To generalise, it seems that the partners' lack of faith in each other led to the decision to avoid a major investment, which led to the poor performance and distorted pay-offs, which further enhanced each parent's lack of trust in the other's ability and commitment. This vicious circle steadily worsened until each venture collapsed.

A close comparison of these two ventures allows some interesting observations to be made concerning joint venture longevity. In spite of similar circumstances, one of these ventures did not collapse until about three years after the other. More surprisingly, the Baker venture, which lasted longer was that in which the American parent was performing most poorly as a subcontractor — not even meeting the landed costs of equipment imported from Germany. I believe the reasons for the differences in longevity are closely related to differences in the attitudes and objectives of the German firms when the ventures were formed and to the options open to the Germans in each case if they pulled out of the venture.

Prior to entering the joint venture Kohmag was earning a good profit supplying the US market from Germany. It had a healthy market share, although this was being threatened through rising prices which were the result of the increases in value of the deutschmark versus the dollar. The specific objective of entering the joint venture was to lower manufacturing costs to a level 30-40 per cent below the landed cost of Kohmag equipment in the US at a high cost, Kohmag's overall profit from supplying the US market was sharply reduced. Baker, on the other hand, had never had any independent success in the US market. It needed Amcoal's marketing contacts just to survive. By the late 1970s Baker executives were probably unsure of the extent to which they still needed Amcoal's help, but that was quite a different position from that of Kohmag who knew they had enough marketing skills to operate on their own. Thus, Kohmag executives were less likely to be tolerant of poor manufacturing performance.

Even when it was clear that both ventures were performing poorly, the German parents faced quite a different degrees of uncertainty. In Kohmag's case, the joint venture was remarkable for its lack of 'joint-ness'. It had acquired no employees from Amcoal and looked and operated exactly as it had when it was a wholly owned subsidiary. Thus, if Kohmag were to buy back Amcoal's 50 per cent of the venture, Kohmag would be in control of a known operation. Leaving the joint venture would mean an increase in certainty of their US operations. For Baker, the opposite was true. Any move to abandon their joint venture would result in great uncertainty. Many of the employees in the venture came from Amcoal. Even the general manager and technical director, who had been hired by Baker, had been given only six months' training before being sent to the US. They were hardly 'Baker men'. If it came to a choice between working for Baker and working for Amcoal, it was not obvious which they would choose. There was also the question of marketing help which the general manager received from Amcoal executives. How well could they do without it? Withdrawal from this joint venture would not be easy or without risk for Baker.

My conclusion is that Baker executives would work much harder to make their joint venture succeed than would Kohmag executives. They were getting more benefit from the connection with Amcoal, and they did not have a clear-cut method for leaving if times got tough. It was not a difference in performance which allowed one joint venture to survive longer than the other, but rather a difference in attitude on the part of the German parent.

Conclusion

These two failures were very frustrating and expensive for the three firms involved. In addition to direct financial losses, a lot of what could prove to be precious time was wasted. The German firms will be making their major entry into the US market unfortunately late, although Kohmag will be all right, if its manager's forecasts are to be believed. The US company appears to have lost out on this new market completely, as it still does not have the technology necessary to enter it.

These cases demonstrate rather dramatically that there are many ways for a joint venture to go bad. In both situations the venture appeared to make sense, and the chosen parties seemed appropriate. Also, the ventures were reasonably managed, especially considering the complexity in which their general managers were operating. I have argued in this chapter that each venture was undermined by one faulty investment decision, in which the managers involved followed a too conservative course of action because they were not fully confident of one another. Clearly all three components have to be right if the venture is to succeed; the basic situation has to be appropriate, including the choice of partner, the design of the venture has to be right and its management has to be good. If any one of these components is wrong, the venture can easily be lost.

8 A MANAGERIAL PERSPECTIVE

This final chapter is being written six months after the rest of the book. It offers both a managerial perspective and summary of the major ideas in the book and identifies issues which remain unresolved. Following the completion of the first seven chapters of the book, my article 'How to Make a Global Joint Venture Work' appeared in the *Harvard Business Review*,[1] which led to my involvement in the design of several new joint ventures being established by very large multinational firms. As a result, I experienced first hand the uncertainties and concerns of managers making key decisions in the creation of significant ventures. I was forced to evaluate my work in an action setting and to decide which principles were most important. The priorities which resulted are contained in this chapter. Through my close identification with the managers involved in these projects, I also began to gain new perspectives on some familiar issues, such as the difficulty of playing the role of a passive partner, even when one is intellectually convinced that such a stance makes sense.

The Decision to Proceed with a Venture

The Carrot

How big a 'carrot' is the joint venture going after? No matter how carefully put together, joint ventures do create stress and strain between parents, and there will be times when only the prospect of a *high* potential pay-off will keep both partners working. The more 'shared' the management of the venture promises to be, the more difficult it will be to manage, and the better the prospective pay-off should be. If the pay-off to either parent is marginal, I would question the wisdom of forming the venture.

It is, of course, rather difficult to estimate how well any new venture will perform in advance of its creation. Some firms, excited by the prospect of entering a joint venture, spend a lot of effort designing its internal operation and relationship with its parents but are less scrupulous about examining the market, the competition, the venture's strengths and weaknesses, and prospects. If anything, such an analysis should be done more carefully for a joint venture than a wholly owned

119

subsidiary. My conclusion is that both the internal organisational relationships in a joint venture and its external competitive posture should be planned in advance, with a very high degree of care and attention.

A final comment relates to the question of designing pay-offs for each partner. It is not enough that the venture itself is going after a high pay-off, it must also distribute the wealth it creates to the parents in what they perceive to be a fair proportion, considering the relative skills and resources which they have devoted to the venture. As explained in Chapter Four, there are a great many techniques by which parents can capture the economic benefits created by a venture, and an even greater number of ways in which real or perceived injustices can arise. This is another area of joint venture design requiring careful attention to detail because, once established, these pay-off agreements are difficult to change and have the potential to be very disruptive.

Do You Need a Partner? For How Long?

Quite a few joint ventures are formed to solve what are, for at least one of the partners, temporary problems. Factors which seem compelling at the time, such as a lack of knowledge with respect to the intended market, insufficient financial resources or a desire for quick market penetration using a partner's distribution system, often lead firms to enter joint ventures which they later regret. If your need for a partner is, or could be, short term in nature. I would suggest one of the following courses of action.

1. *Get the assistance you need through a more flexible mechanism than a joint venture.* Analyse carefully the reasons why you do not feel you can exploit the business situation in question on your own. If it is technology you lack, and you have the technical competence to tell the difference between a good and bad licensor, look hard for a licence agreement. The major advantage of a licence agreement is that you will retain a much higher degree of managerial flexibility than you would with a joint venture. As discussed at length in Chapter Six, the choice between a joint venture and a licence agreement should be based on the relationship between the skills you currently have and those you need for the new business.

If you need a partner to provide local managers for the venture, look carefully to see if you can hire such managers on the open market. If it's his financing you need, see if there isn't another way you can arrange it. Forming a joint venture, particularly with a partner who is not willing to play a passive role, is a very expensive way of obtaining either money or managers.

2. *Postpone the venture until you can undertake it alone.* If you currently employ managers who could manage the new project but you can't spare them from your existing operation, or if you can't currently finance the new operation because of expansion at home, you might consider waiting until you do have the resources to do it alone. I realise that the competitive situation often makes it seem imperative to move immediately, but I suspect that circumstances are often less compelling than they appear and that opportunities do continue to arise for most companies.

Waiting, however, is no solution for some problems. If you need a partner because of your lack of knowledge of a market or country, waiting to enter a joint venture is unlikely to make much difference. Ironically, the best way to become familiar with the country may be through a joint venture – thus soon eliminating your need for the venture.

3. *Set up the venture on a project basis, with a definite termination date.* Projects are often successfully managed as joint ventures. Because a project's objectives are usually very clear cut and often divisible into discrete component parts which the various partners will undertake, the major management decisions in a project can often be made before it is established. The question is whether or not other joint venture business situations can be set up in a manner similar to projects. Some attention has been given to the possibility of 'fade out' joint ventures for use in developing countries, but there is no reason why such a notion could not apply equally to ventures in developed countries. The idea behind a fade out joint venture is that it would be set up with a pre-planned schedule under which the foreign partner would sell out its interests to the local partner or the local government. The foreign firm might or might not retain a management contract or a technical assistance agreement and might retain a minority (passive) interest in the venture. Guy Meeker, an MBA student at George Washington University, carried out a study to see what large American multinationals operating in Latin America thought of this idea.[2] Thirty-five per cent of his respondents stated that they thought the idea was

acceptable, although only about seven per cent of the 90 responding firms had been actually involved in such an arrangement. The extractive industry was the only one in which more firms favoured the proposal than were against it. This is understandable, as these companies typically find themselves the victims of particularly strong nationalistic sentiments, and also they are exploiting a diminishing resource which would have decreased substantially in value by the time (15 or 20 years is the usual suggested frame of reference) the transfer in ownership would take place. In spite of fairly widespread publicity, this technique for establishing and ending a joint venture has not, to the best of my knowledge, been extensively used.

4. *At the very least, incorporate in the joint venture agreement a clear-cut mechanism for ending the venture.* At the beginning of a joint venture you and your partner will typically anticipate that by pooling your resources you are jointly going to create wealth. At least to some extent you need one another and have shared objectives. However, if you are seriously considering breaking up the venture, the belief that there will be wealth created by the two of you working together, or at least that both of you are required to work together to create the wealth, has died. At this point the issue is the division of rewards, a win/lose game, rather than their creation, which is a win/win game. For this reason, a procedure for ending a joint venture should be devised when it is being set up.

The most usual mechanism used for ending a joint venture is the 'shotgun' buy/sell agreement, under which either party can name a price at which it will buy the other out. The second firm, however, has the option of either selling at this price or buying the first party's shares at the same price. This simple mechanism insures that only fair offers are made, at least as long as both parents are large enough to be capable of buying one another out. There is no doubt that this mechanism can and has worked efficiently to end joint ventures, sometimes to the surprise of firms who thought they were buying 50 per cent of a venture, only to discover they were selling their own half. It is unlikely that firms which cannot run a joint venture on their own would trigger such a mechanism, and this is good, as it means it will not usually be used until one parent is no longer necessary to the successful operation of the venture. Used properly, the buy/sell agreement ends a joint venture efficiently, at a fair price to both parties.

What Kind of Partner Do You Need?

Obviously your partner needs to provide the skills and/or attributes that you require to make a success of the business situation in question. Beyond this simple observation, however, it is difficult to make useful generalisations about the selection of a partner. It is all very well to specify appropriate character traits such as reasonableness, honesty and trustworthiness, but such characteristics do not generally become evident until stressful situations arise, by which time it is too late to do much about your choice of partner. This observation suggests that, other things being equal, you should choose as a partner a firm which you know well from previous dealing. If this is not possible, I would suggest a lengthy courtship period before your agreement is signed, so you will each have a better idea of what you are getting as a partner. Executives tend to see six months as a minimum courtship period.

As I stated in Chapter Four, I would recommend that joint ventures be not formed between firms which differ significantly in size. When one parent is, say, ten times as large as the other, many extra problems arise. Another situation which some executives warn against are joint ventures with governments. Although an increasingly frequent practice, this is an area that has not received attention from researchers, and I know of no studies which address the advisability of forming joint ventures with government agencies. It is an area deserving further study.

As a final word on the decision to go ahead with a joint venture I must emphasise that there are no absolute rights and wrongs. What I have tried to do is point out the factors which seem to increase or decrease the probabilities of success. One can make a success of a venture 'against the odds', just as a 'perfectly' set up joint venture can fail. Unfortunately, in this area, like most others in business, there are no guarantees.

The Major Design Questions

If you decide to go ahead with a joint venture you will be faced with a number of immediate questions. How big will the board be, and who will be on it? Who will be the general manager? What will the venture's organisation chart look like? Where will the function managers come from? Behind each of these primary questions lies a continuing secondary question, namely, who will decide each of these things? More specifically, what will be the role of each parent in the management of the venture?

I have found that joint ventures in which both parents are heavily involved managerially have a much higher failure rate than those in which one or the other dominates. If one parent's skills and judgements are not necessary to the success of the joint venture and if that parent is willing to play a passive role, the prescription is relatively straightforward. Set up a venture dominated by the parent whose skills are critical to its success.

1. Give the board of directors, which will contain executives from each parent, as few decisions to make as possible.
2. Allow the dominant parent to select the general manager — in all probability a current employee. He need not be particularly skilled at managing joint ventures, because this venture will not be very 'joint'.
3. The organisation chart will be designed by the joint venture general manager or his superiors in the dominant parent, and functional managers will be selected from the dominant parent or hired outside as they deem appropriate.
4. As much as possible, the dominant parent will manage the venture as if it were a wholly owned subsidiary.

If, however, one parent's strategic input (but not ongoing operating judgements) is important to the venture, or if one parent without relevant skills nevertheless insists on being involved in the strategic management of the venture, some changes will be required.

1. The board will have to be involved in significant strategic decision making, but do insist that it keep out of operating decisions. There is a strong correlation between a venture general manager's autonomy and joint venture success.
2. The general manager should again be provided by the parent with the relevant operating skills, and he should be an experienced general manager, preferably with joint venture experience. Managing the board of directors will be a significant challenge for him. This job is definitely more difficult than that described earlier.
3. The functional managers should be from the relevant skill parent if possible, with good operational links into that parent. One should try to keep 'informers' from the relatively passive parent to a minimum. More will be said about this in the section which discusses how to be a passive parent.

4. Below the board level, try to manage the venture as a cohesive unit, with links with only one parent. That is, below the general manager level the venture should operate and look like a dominant parent venture. Only above him will the 'joint' aspects of the venture really be seen.

If both parents have relevant operating skills and strategic inputs to make, or if one parent without such skills insists on being involved at both levels, you are in a different managerial situation. (Actually, if one parent without skills insisted on being equally involved at both levels of management, I would recommend that the venture not be formed.) In such a venture, there will be a high potential for conflict and delay at both the board and functional level, as was adequately demonstrated in the early chapters of this book.

1. The board's role will be similar to that just described. Again try to give the general manager as much autonomy as possible. The more decisions that have to be brought to the board, the more difficult his position will be.
2. The general manager must have previous joint venture general manager experience. His job will be extremely difficult. See Chapter Five for a discussion of ambiguity, allegiance, trust and autonomy.
3. The functional managers will come from both parents. Such a situation can be divisive, and is one reason a good general manager is called for.
4. Over time, a successful general manager will build the joint venture up as a unit *separate* from its parents. Managers will come to identify with it, not the parent they come from. Allow this to happen, do not keep rotating these people in and out of the parent. As the joint venture develops its own skills, its dependencies will lessen. Independent joint ventures are more successful than shared management ones.

A Note on Being a Passive Parent

The most significant finding of this research is that joint ventures are more likely to succeed if one parent has the skills required to manage the venture alone and is allowed to do so by the other parent. I have found that firms accept this notion readily, as it fits with their own experience, but even so they have difficulty taking a 'hands off' approach to the venture if the role of passive parent logically falls to them. One multinational whose European subsidiary had been performing poorly decided to merge it with a very successful local competitor, to form a 50–50 joint venture. The corporate multinational managers wanted to force the new joint venture general manager (previously the manager of the local competitor) to hire their subsidiary general manager and a number of his functional managers, thus limiting his autonomy from the outset and loading the venture with possibly marginal performers. All of this was in spite of the fact that the multinational managers stated that they had a very high degree of respect for the venture's general manager and were counting on his expertise to make the venture a success. Obtaining his services was in fact a major motivation for the venture!

The reason for this and similar behaviour is that multinationals, operating in areas in which they don't know the culture particularly well, are afraid of being cheated by their local partner. They feel strongly that they need someone in the venture that they can trust to tell them what's really going on. Having a couple of executives on the venture's board of directors is not sufficient, because they will only be shown what the dominant parent chooses to show them and will only hear what the dominant parent chooses to tell them.

I believe that the solution for firms who cannot bring themselves to trust their partners totally is to try and find ways of getting the 'comfort level' they need without doing things (like imposing managers) that will impair the venture's chances of success. There are several possibilities. As a basic precaution, ensure that the venture's auditors are a firm in which you have confidence. Beyond this, if you have a useful strategic input to make because you know the business or venture in question well (this was the case in the European venture just described), then suggest that an executive committee of the venture's board be formed. This committee, comprising one member from each parent and the joint venture general manager, would meet and communicate frequently. It would allow the passive parent a 'window' on the venture, but in a non-destructive, a hopefully useful fashion. If, on the other hand, the passive parent has no knowledge or skills useful to the venture but needs the comfort of knowing 'what's going on' on a regular basis, the least obtrusive solution may be to place a junior employee in the venture for 'training', possibly in the finance area. He can report home on a regular basis, but will be at a low enough level that his divided loyalties may not cause a problem. As a final note,

I would urge passive parents to exhibit a higher degree of trust in their partners. By entering into the venture you are showing a high degree of confidence in your partner's competence. Why then start to hedge? The joint venture is in his area of business, not yours. If his honesty is in question you should not have formed the venture in the first place.

Joint Ventures in Developing Countries

Probably the greatest limitation of this research is that it has dealt virtually exclusively with joint ventures in developed countries. Do the conclusions also apply to ventures in developing countries? I don't believe there is enough evidence yet available to answer this question. What appears to be one of the most interesting studies on joint ventures in developing countries done thus far is currently in progress at the University of Western Ontario. A working paper just published by Paul Beamish and Harry Lane provides a preliminary report on their work, which examines the performance of joint ventures in developing countries.[3] In their preliminary sample of 34 ventures involved Canadian and developing country partners, the authors found that an astounding 61 per cent were considered by the Canadian partner to have unsatisfactory performance. In sharp contrast to my sample, none of the ventures were equally owned, and in 79 per cent the multinational firm held a minority ownership position. (Apparently this high proportion of minority foreign ownership positions is typical of ventures in developing countries.) Over half of the ventures in the Beamish/Lane sample were formed because of government suasion or legislation, and approximately 30 per cent were formed with the local government as the multinational's partner.

In examining the performance of these 34 ventures, Beamish and Lane found no clear relationship between success/failure and the variables which other researchers have found important in explaining joint venture performance in developed countries. No consistent pattern was observed between success and level of technology, export orientation, ownership level, government versus private partners, staffing with expatriate versus local managers, or type of management control. They also reported that mixing managers from the two parent companies together seemed to cause no particular problems, somewhat to my surprise. As a result of these negative findings, Beamish and Lane concluded that a different set of factors must be important to the success of joint ventures in developing countries than those in developed countries. They chose to examine the level and nature of each partner's need and commitment to the venture, and found that these factors did explain the performance differences of the ventures in their sample.

Need and commitment are difficult, intangible variables to measure, and it is too early to assess fully the Beamish/Lane attempt to come to grips with them. What they are testing is the notion that if a major need for one's partner is a short-term need, such as speeding one's entry into a new market, failure of the joint venture is more likely than if the need is longer term. Of course, the longevity of a firm's need for its partner is a function of its own learning ability, and this tends to be a difficult thing to forecast. How long will you need a partner? How long will your partner need you? Once the need is gone, the venture becomes very fragile, a fact of life reiterated more than once in this book and likely to be reaffirmed by Beamish and Lane.

Reviewing this research reminds me of the fact that there are situations in which shared management ventures are the best available solution, an observation made in Chapter Four but which may have been understated subsequently in my desire to encourage firms to move toward dominant parent ventures. Shared management ventures are necessary when neither parent has all of the skills and knowledge required to manage the venture alone. This, I suspect, is often the case in developing country ventures. The foreign firm would not have sufficient knowledge to operate in the local environment, whereas the local firm cannot manage the technology on its own.

The Final Word

If you accept the notion that joint ventures, when freely formed, (i.e. without the interference of governments) are solutions to what are essentially temporary problems, then the solutions should be temporary as well. I consider the motivation for a joint venture to be largely temporary, because the knowledge or assets which a firm acquires from its partner can usually be learned or acquired over time. Joint ventures built around projects are even more obviously temporary. So most joint ventures will and should come to an end. But a successful end, not a messy one! The best antidote to an acrimonious termination is to have a joint venture which performs well. It is easier to divide the spoils from a victory, than to allocate the blame and loss from a defeat. Hence this book. The best way to solve the 'end game' of a joint venture is to design and manage it well in the first place. Good hunting!

Notes

1. Killing, J.P., 'How to Make a Global Joint Venture Work', *Harvard Business Review*, May–June 1982.

2. Meeker, G.B., 'Fade Out Joint Venture: Can it Work for Latin America?' *Inter-American Economic Affairs*, vol. XXIV, No. 4, Spring 1971, pp. 25–42.

3. Beamish, P. and Lane, H.W., 'Need, Commitment, and the Performance of Joint Ventures in Developing Countries', *Working Paper Series No. 330*, School of Business Administration, University of Western Ontario, Canada, July 1982.

BIBLIOGRAPHY

Adler, Lee and Hlavacek, J.D., 'Joint Ventures for Product Innovation', Study done for the American Management Association (Amacon, New York, 1976)

Beamish, P. and Lane, H.W., 'Need, Commitment, and the Performance of Joint Ventures in Developing Countries', working paper series no. 330, School of Business Administration, University of Western Ontario, Canada, July 1982

Berg, S.V. and Friedman, P., 'Joint Ventures in American Industry' (part one), *Mergers and Acquisitions*, vol. 13, no. 2, Summer 1978

Dang, Tran, 'Ownership, Control and Performance of the Multinational Corporation: A Study of US Wholly-owned Subsidiaries and Joint Ventures in the Philippines and Taiwan', PhD thesis, University of California, 1977

Davies, H., 'Technology Transfer Through Commercial Transaction', *Journal of Industrial Economics*, December 1977

Ducker, P., *Management: Tasks, Responsibilities, Practices* (Harper and Row, New York, 1973)

Franko, L.G., *The European Multinationals* (Harper and Row, London, 1976)

—— *Joint Venture Survival in Multinational Corporations* (Praeger Publishers, New York, 1971)

Friedmann, W.G. and Kalmanoff, G., *Joint International Business Ventures* (Columbia University Press, New York, 1961)

—— and Begiun, J.P., *Joint International Business Ventures in Developing Countries* (Columbia University Press, New York, 1971)

Good, Loretta, 'United States Joint Ventures and Manufacturing Firms in Monterrey, Mexico: Comparative Styles of Management', PhD thesis, Cornell University, 1972

Janger, Allen R., *Organization of International Joint Ventures* (The Conference Board, New York, 1980)

—— *International Joint Ventures* (The Conference Board, New York, 1980)

Killing, J. Peter, 'How to Make a Global Venture Work', *Harvard Business Review*, May–June, 1982

—— 'Manufacturing Under Licence', *Business Quarterly*, Winter, 1977

LaPaslombara, J.H., and Blauk, S., *Multinational Corporations in Comparative Perspective* (The Conference Board, New York, 1977)

Meeker, G.B., 'Fade Out Joint Venture: Can it Work for Latin America?' *Inter-American Economic Affairs*, vol. XXIV, no. 4, Spring, 1971

'Mergers and Acquisitions: The Journal of Corporate Venture', published quarterly by Information for Industry Inc., McLean, Virginia

Rafii, Farshad, 'Joint Ventures and the Transfer of Technology to Iran: The Impact of Foreign Control', unpublished DBA thesis, Harvard University, 1978

Raveed, Sion, 'Joint Ventures Between US Multinational Firms and Host Governments in Selected Developing Countries: A Case Study of Costa Rica, Trinidad and Venezuela', DBA thesis, Indiana University, 1976

Renforth, William, 'A Comparative Study of Joint International Business Ventures with Family Firm or Non-family Partners: The Caribbean Community', DBA thesis, Indiana University, 1974

Schaan, J.L., 'Parent Control and Joint Venture Success: The Case of Mexico', PhD thesis, University of Western Ontario, London, Ontario 1983

Stopford, John M. and Wells, Jr, Louis T., *Managing the Multinational Enterprise* (Basic Books, New York, 1972)

'Technology Acquisition: License Agreement or Joint Venture?', *Columbia Journal of World Business*, Fall, 1980

Tomlinson, J.W.C., and Thompson, M., *A Study of Canadian Joint Ventures in Mexico, Interim Report*, Department of Industry, Trade and Commerce, Technology Branch, Canada. Undated

—— and Willie, C.S.W., *Cross Impact Stimulation of the Joint Venture Process in Mexico*, Department of Industry, Trade and Commerce, Office of Science and Technology, Ottawa, Canada, December 1978

—— and Hills, S.M., *Potential Opportunities for Canadian Joint Ventures in Venezuela and Columbia*, Department of Industry, Trade and Commerce, Ottawa, Canada, 1978

Wrigley, L., 'Divisional Autonomy and Diversification', PhD thesis, Harvard Business School. Unpublished

Note: Many of the references relating to joint ventures in developing countries were taken from the thesis of Jean-Louis Schaan, 'Parent Control and Joint Venture Success: The Case of Mexico' (University of Western Ontario), which was in the final stages of preparation in February 1983.

INDEX

DATE DUE

DATE DUE			
OCT 24 '91			
DEC 23 '92			
MAY 31 '93			
MAY 31 '94			
JUL 31 '95			
DEC 19 '95			
APR 23 2000			